The Shape of Things to Come[1]

The EU Future Group

'Every object the individual uses, every transaction they make and almost everywhere they go will create a detailed digital record. This will generate a wealth of information for public security organisations, and create huge opportunities for more effective and productive public security efforts.'
EU Council Presidency Paper

Tony Bunyan

SPOKESMAN BOOKS
for
STATEWATCH

© Statewatch

First published in 2009 by
Spokesman Books
Russell House, Bulwell Lane
Nottingham NG6 0BT
England
Phone 0115 9708318   Fax: 0115 9420433
e-mail: elfeuro@compuserve.com
www.spokesmanbooks.com

ISBN 13 978 085124 760 1

A CIP Catalogue is available from the British Library.

Printed by the Russell Press Ltd., (phone 0115 9784505)

CONTENTS

1

Introduction

This book looks at the ideology in the Future Group report, *Freedom, Security and Privacy – the area of European Home Affairs*. The European Union is currently developing a new five year strategy for justice and home affairs and security policy for 2009-2014. The proposals set out by the shadowy 'Future Group' include a range of extremely controversial measures including techniques and technologies of surveillance and enhanced cooperation with the United States.[2]

This book examines the proposals of the Future Group and their relation to existing and planned EU policies. It shows how European governments and EU policy-makers are pursuing unfettered powers to access and gather masses of personal data on the everyday life of everyone – on the grounds that we can all be safe and secure from perceived 'threats'.

The Council of the European Union's 'Future Group' presented its final report at the Justice and Home Affairs Council's July 2008 meeting. This will lead to a new Justice and Home Affairs Programme for 2010-2014, following the 'Tampere' programme (1999-2004) and the 'Hague' programme 2005-2009. The final programme will be proposed by the European Commission, then amended and adopted by the Council. It will set out a detailed programme for both new measures and practices for the five-year period.

The 'Timetable' indicates that the new five year plan will be adopted under the Swedish Council Presidency in the second half of 2009 – the 'Stockholm programme' maybe.[3] The final report is intended to be the basis of a proposal from the European Commission and, unlike the processes for the adoption of the Tampere and Hague programmes, it also suggests that the European Parliament will be consulted – but, as usual, the Council of the European Union (the 27 governments) will have the final say on its content.

The Future Group was set up in January 2007. Ministers had agreed to a German Presidency proposal at the informal Justice and Home Affairs (JHA) meeting in Dresden on 14-16 January 2007, and later 'in the margins' of the JHA Council on 14 February 2007.[4] Its final report is from the 'Informal High Level Advisory Group on the Future of European Home Affairs Policy' and is entitled: *Freedom, Security and Privacy – European Home Affairs in an Open World*. A separate report was also published on justice.[5] The Tampere and Hague programmes were concerned with both home affairs and justice, so this separation is unusual but deliberate. In many member states the Justice Ministries are often perceived as being more 'liberal' as they cover peoples' rights in the criminal justice system, whereas Interior Ministries are more concerned with the agencies that exercise coercive powers over citizens and migrants.

The 'Future Group' meetings were co-chaired by the Interior Minister for the Council Presidency and the Vice-Chair of the European Commission (Mr Frattini, before he went back to Italy to become Foreign Minister in Berlusconi's far-right government). Its members were the Interior Ministries of two 'trios' (two sets of three), as they are called, of Council Presidencies.[6] The first trio is Germany, Portugal and Slovenia and the second trio is France (current Council President), Czech Republic and Sweden plus a representative from the third trio of the next three Presidencies – Spain, Belgium and Hungary. Another 'participant' was a 'common law observer' – the United Kingdom – which submitted a paper that had nothing to do with common law. Also on the Group as 'observers' were the President of the LIBE (Civil Liberties) Committee of the European Parliament and a 'representative' of the Secretariat General of the Council (Director General for Justice and Home Affairs).[7] The Group held six meetings.

Changing terminology and ideology in EU state-building

It may be pure chance that there are only five references in the report to the area of freedom, security and justice and thirteen to the area of European home affairs. Certainly the sub-title of *Freedom, Security and Privacy* suggests a new and, on examination, tokenistic notion of privacy.[8]

Noticeable, too, is the shift from references to 'law enforcement agencies' (LEAs), as requiring this or that power, to 'public security organisations' including LEAs but not limited to them. This is a logical shift now that the internal-external-security-nexus is explicitly the dominant concept; i.e. strengthening the powers of *all* security agencies, not just those dealing with terrorism and serious crime.

From Tampere to Hague

In October 1999, the Council (EU governments) adopted the Tampere programme covering the whole of justice and home affairs for the period 1999-2004.[9] The final text, adopted on 16 October 1999, was not available until the morning of that day and was adopted a few hours later. There was no involvement of national or European parliaments in drafting the text, nor could civil society discuss and comment.[10]

It was always a bit of a mystery as to who drew up the draft text that was taken to Tampere. There had been an informal JHA Council in Turku, Finland, in the spring where little if any detail emerged. The JHA Council meeting in Luxembourg in June added little, and the Finnish Prime Minister conducted a *'tour des capitals'*.

It has emerged that the key players were Charles Elsen, then acting Director General in the Council Secretariat for Justice and Home Affairs, aided by the late Adrian Fortescue, who headed a JHA 'task force' in the Commission. An article by Elsen for the Academy of European Law (Trier) says, extraordinarily, that:

'it was decided to involve the working groups and the Justice and Home Affairs Council in this work as little as possible.'[11]

He says this was because they did not want 'technical ministers' (i.e. Interior/Home Ministers and Justice Ministers) involved as 'heads of government are capable of demonstrating more ambition than experts' – and heads of government, not being experts, would be dependent on Elsen who took part in the Finnish PM's 'tour' and 'participated actively in the preparations'.

The 'Hague programme' was also negotiated in secret meetings, a text was available a couple of weeks before it was adopted on 5 November 2004, as an 'A' point – simply nodded through – at the European Council (meetings of Prime Ministers). Again, there was no time for any democratic input.

2

What is already planned
or being discussed

To appreciate what is 'new' in the Future Group report a quick resumé of what is already in the pipeline or planned is necessary.

In 2006, a directive on the mandatory retention of all communications data across the EU was adopted. Service providers are obliged to keep and give agencies access to records of all phone calls, mobile phone calls (and their location), faxes, e-mails and internet usage. This year most EU states that had not done so, are implementing this at national level. In short, records of all communications by everyone in the EU are held and can be accessed by agencies in connection with 'serious crime, as defined by each Member State in its national law', which varies from member state to member state or for suspicion of a 'serious crime'.[12]

In 2004, a regulation on EU passports required the taking of fingerprints (biometrics) from all applying for one. Again, there was a time lag in the implementation at national level. But, from 2009 onwards, millions of people across the EU will have to attend special centres to be interviewed (to prove who they are), then compulsorily fingerprinted.

The fingerprinting of everyone applying for a visa to visit the EU from third countries is already underway, and fingerprinting of resident third country nationals has been agreed. Discussions are underway on extending the taking of fingerprints for national ID cards as these are used for travel within the Schengen area.

It is sobering to note that the mass surveillance of all telecommunications, and mass fingerprinting of all, are two proposals that have not been proposed in the USA. Thus the EU is set to become the most surveilled place in the world.

EU laws on driving licences have been harmonised so that licences have to be renewed initially every 10 years, with the option for every five years. In the UK a driving licence is held from passing the test until the age of 70 (when it can be renewed with a doctor's letter). Renewing the licence every 10 years will mean the 'chip' and the data on it can be updated and adapted.

In the UK a National Health database will hold the records of all 60 million people with over 350,000 'clinicians' having access – as will police and security agencies. The EU is planning a new EU Health Card and argues for the benefits of being able to travel anywhere with your medical details available.

The EU is also keen on 'e-government' cards, and much research is being conducted. 'E-government' gives people access to state services where they have to prove who they are, for example, to get medical or hospital treatment, local government services such as libraries, getting social and unemployment benefits, and so on.

The day may not be far off when all these state-run systems will be put on 'one-card': passport, ID card, driving licence, health record and e-government.

The Schengen Information System (SIS) is to be upgraded to hold more categories of data (including fingerprints and DNA), and access to all the data is to be extended to all agencies (police, immigration and customs).[13] SIS II is to share a 'common technical platform' with VIS (Visa Information System) for the policing of visitors – thus SIS II/VIS will become a dedicated surveillance tool.[14]

Discussions to create an EU-PNR (passenger name record) system are under way. In June 2008, the Council threw the Commission proposal out and, in the autumn, it will draw up its own draft. A number of governments do not like limiting the use of data to terrorism and organised crime, and want to extend the proposal's scope from just in and out of the EU to travel between EU states and even within each state. The same view also supports extending the scope from air travel to land and sea travel too.

An EU entry-exit system is planned for third country nationals entering with visas, and those without visas too, as is an EU version of an Electronic System for Travel Authorisation (ESTA). The former proposal includes the automated checking of EU citizens – that is, passports and biometrics (fingerprints) to be checked by 'machines' not people. The EU-PNR exit-entry system and ESTA will put the EU on the same footing as the USA.

The Prüm Treaty, agreed by 17 EU member states, has lead to the incorporation of the policing aspects into EU law (the automated exchange of DNA, fingerprint and vehicle data) thus applying across all 27 member states. The immigration aspects, including the use of air marshals, are being adopted by the signatory states.

The Lisbon Treaty will include extensive increases in operational police cooperation at the EU level, and the creation of the Committee on Internal Security (COSI).[15]

A good summary of the measures adopted in the wake of the Madrid bombings in 2004 and the extent to which they concern 'terrorism' is available in Statewatch's Scoreboard.[16]

In June 2008, the EU agreed, in principle, on the Returns Directive under which those found to be 'illegally' resident in the EU are to be rounded up and held in detention centres for as long as 18 months before being deported to their assumed country of origin. Some defined as 'illegal' will have been in the EU for days or weeks, others may have been here for years with their children being 'second-generation'. The directive makes no distinction – they are all 'illegal'.

At the same time, 'legal migration' is to be encouraged. Due to the EU's ageing population it needs skilled labour from the third world to maintain its standard of living – and its continued exploitation of the third world's resources.

The EU-USA nexus developed apace after 11 September (see case study below).

Also relevant is the extension of NATO's role beyond the bounds of Europe in 2002. Twenty-one EU member states are in NATO, and most are involved in the war in Afghanistan.[17]

Finally, the European Security Research Agenda is an important part of the background to the Future Group report.[18] As the TNI/Statewatch report, *Arming Big Brother*, observes:

'Myriad local and global surveillance systems; the introduction of biometric identifiers; radio-frequency identification (RFID), electronic tagging and satellite monitoring; "less-lethal weapons"; paramilitary equipment for public order and crisis management; and the militarization of border controls – technological advances in law enforcement are often welcomed uncritically but rarely are these technologies neutral, in either application or effect. Military organisations dominate research and development in these areas under the banner of "dual-use" technology, avoiding both the constraints and controversies of the arms trade. Tomorrow's technologies of control quickly become today's political imperative; contentious policies appear increasingly irresistible.'

3

The Future Group's 'warm-up' session and documents submitted

The ideas submitted to the Future Group are more explicit than the final report, which often lapses into generalities or obscure language. The main proposals are summarised here.[19]

The summary of the 'Warm-up session', held in Eltville, Germany on 20-21 May, is interesting. Commission Vice-President Frattini told the meeting that the 2008 Commission 'Scoreboard' on the Hague programme would show that achievements were lower than in 2005:

'only 53% of measures have been achieved.'

Frattini then said:

*'the overarching future challenge is the **further development of new technologies and their link to financing at EU level**, including in the area of security research and structural funds. Databases and new technologies will play a central role in further developing JLS JHA policies in the areas of border management, migration, fight against organised crime and global terrorism.'* (emphasis in original)

As we shall see later, the use of 'new technologies' and EU funding for standardised systems at national level is in the final report. He also drew attention to 'security research' including the creation of the European Security Research and Innovation Forum (ESRIF). They had to find, he said:

'a new balance between the right to security and the protection of fundamental rights ... There is a need to overcome the traditional dogma of seeing collective security and individual freedom as two opposed concepts which exclude each other. Individual rights can only flourish in an atmosphere of collective security.'

To which one can respond, that if 'collective security' demands the surveillance of all movements, all telecommunications, and the collection of all the fingerprints of everyone living in the EU, there can be no individual freedom, except that sanctioned by the state. 'Freedom' is not just about rights, it is also the freedom 'from' state surveillance and control. Put another way, if 'collective security' requires the state, in 'the name of all', to set the limits, boundaries and sanctions of all our actions, it is a recipe not for 'freedom' but enslavement.

'Upcoming' priorities, Frattini said, included:

'the wider use of phone-tapping and CCTV'

11

and, a 'multilateral legal initiative for a new definition of terrorism' on which talks had been started with the USA and Russia – this is a reference to the blocked discussions in the UN where the EU and USA, amongst others, refuse to include any reference to 'state terrorism'.

The co-chair, Minister Frieden, from Luxembourg, offered the following proposals for discussion:

> *'Ministers of Interior should give themselves an "EU Internal Security policy" by defining the operational priorities of its actions every two years.'*

At least the Minister is honest. EU Interior Ministers should 'give themselves' powers to lay down plans for EU-wide operations. In a phrase echoing through the Future Group's deliberations he said:

> *'Member States should* ***"pool their own sovereignty"*** *and not fear the EU.'* (emphasis in original)

This 'pooling their sovereignty' is a euphemism for giving more power to the EU and Interior Ministers 'giving themselves' the power to decide policy. While Europol should become:

> *'a real European Criminal Police, provided with a common investigative structure'*

and 'multinational police offices' should be set up, and 'coordinated at EU level', together with, in the long run,:

> *'a European Border Police ... Multinational teams should be put in place so as to run EU inspections at the borders ...'*

The Minister also proposed that a 'real' European Police Academy should be created (in place of CEPOL) and financed by the EU, with 'a common curricula for Member States police officers', together with 'European Refugee and Asylum Centres', and that the implementation of the 'principle of availability', under the Prüm Treaty, was 'just a first step'.

The discussions on the co-chairs' ideas, for which there was much support, included the following points which were placed on record:
– 'The EU should fully exploit the new technologies in security matters and adjust itself to the digital era';
– pass 'all responsibilities for border control to FRONTEX' and in the long run to a European Border Guard;
– third countries: 'at difficult border-crossing points and areas'

12

deploying 'permanent European Reinforcement Teams', for example at the border of Libya and Niger/Chad;
– a *'permanent operational group of immigration officers ... to carry out operations in countries of origin and European borders at any time';*
– FRONTEX could do more 'in the autonomous organisation of return flights to third countries';
– *'migration risks could be reduced by introducing an automated border control system, e.g. for bona-fide travellers and EU citizens';*
– as 'harmonious parts of a global approach' the 'e-border' concept (originating in the UK) was endorsed, including 'the creation of an integrated surveillance system for maritime as well as land borders' and 'entry-exit' control systems. Together with the 'four-tier access control model', which in lay person's language means measures in third countries (including regional border management), neighbouring countries, border controls (risk analyses, checks and surveillance) and 'control measures within the area of free movement' (e.g. returns flights).

Migration and border management

Three papers on migration and border management were submitted to the group, though these issues were also raised in others.[20] An 'Introductory document' submitted was on 'Modernising European border and visa management'. This repeats the EU mantra of:

> *'striking a balance between citizens' needs for freedom and their security needs'*

and it welcomes the establishment of FRONTEX, the introduction of rapid border intervention teams (RABITS), a 'coastal patrol network in the south Mediterranean area', and the development of an 'Integrated Border Management concept'. These go hand-in-hand with the:

> *'development of a common European Security Strategy which is aimed, in particular,* at **forming a "ring" of responsibly governed countries from the EU's eastern borders to the Mediterranean** *(adopted by the European Council in December 2006).'* (emphasis added)

Under the heading 'challenges to internal security' the introductory document says that:

> *'Europe will increasingly become a region of destination for worldwide illegal migration, organised crime and international drug-trafficking and a target of terrorist attacks.'*

There is no mention of climate change, global financial crises (caused by the West), wars started by the West (Iraq), or poverty and displacement caused by Western (especially EU and USA) multinational interests, and persecution by third world states supported by the West.

There is, though, a need for 'synergies' between 'checks on persons and checks on goods' by border police and customs, 'risk profiles in visa-issuing procedures', making use of 'technological advances' for 'entry-exit' procedures, 'e.g. by linkage of the registers on third country nationals staying in Member States', a role for FRONTEX 'as regards cooperation with third countries … in the context of joint return operations' and, finally, agreements to be concluded with third countries with the possibility of:

> *'pre-border checks to be carried out in third countries under an anticipatory strategy.'*

A paper from Portugal and the Czech Republic on a 'Comprehensive European Migration Policy' speaks of:

> *'well managed immigration in 2014. While remaining faithful to European values.'*

As 'European values' on immigration, since 1990, have re-defined the Geneva Convention to greatly restrict the original commitment to refugees in EU policies, one can only conclude, as in so many areas, 'EU values' are re-shaped to match the prevailing political wind.[21] Perhaps this is because 'enhanced citizens' trust' is dependent on:

> *'the assurance that migration occurs … within the law and that it is in conformity with Europe' interests and identity.'*

The EU's new priority is 'legal migration' to meet each 'Member States' labour needs' and their 'integration capacity' while at the same time conducting a 'relentless fight against illegal immigration', 'illegal employment' and 'deepening' the relationship with 'countries of origin and transit'. In the latter context this paper asks:

> *'How can we solve the impasse caused by non-compliance with Article 13 of the Cotonou agreement by third countries.'*

The Cotonou agreement with African, Caribbean and Pacific (ACP) states is one under which the EU wants to send back everyone said to have come from these countries or transited through them.

A third, slightly more thoughtful paper from Sweden and the Czech Republic finds no echoes in the Future report.[22]

Tony Bunyan

UK paper on 'Mobility, Security and Privacy'

Although the UK was not a member of the Future Group, it did participate as an 'Observer' representing 'common law' countries, and submitted a rather strident paper.[23] 'Improving security' in an:

> *'increasingly mobile society require(s) personal data from travellers in advance of their journeys and to strengthen borders and reduce crossing points.'*

The UK paper does not say 'in advance' of 'all' journeys, but this is what it is arguing for in the negotiations on the proposed EU-Passenger Name Record system. The reference to 'reduce crossing points' (i.e. official points where borders are crossed) would have a major effect on the rest of the EU.[24] It also perversely argues that 'E-borders' – where in time all journeys by air, sea and land are recorded, stored and shared – creates 'a secure environment for EU citizens to enjoy their mobility'. The 'mobility' referred to is the much lauded 'freedom of movement' in the EU. Yet it was just over ten years ago when this 'freedom' meant the freedom to travel without being checked or controlled.[25]

In coded language the UK paper alludes to an impending problem. From 2009, millions of people in the EU are going to be fingerprinted if they want a new passport (or lose their old one).[26] The 'biometric fingerprints' will be stored on an embedded chip in the passport. This will allow their identity to be checked either 'one-to-one' for 'verification' or 'one-to-many' (against the whole database) for 'identification'. Such checks will be fine if a UK passport-holder is re-entering the country, as they can be 'identified' against the national database. German or French or Italian border officials can carry out a 'one-to-one' check, that the person standing in front of them is the same person as in the photo, and they can take their fingerprints to check against those on the passport 'chip', but they cannot 'identify' ('one-to-many') them unless they have access to the UK database. That is why the UK paper calls for the effective:

> *'linking of databases in such as way that one State may easily obtain information in the database of another.'*

It also raises the rather urgent issue – given the timetable – of the compatibility of:

> *'forms of identification from one State with the verification technology in others, for example, biometric passports and machine readers at immigration posts.'*

It appears that so far there has been no plan, no coordination across

15

the EU, to make sure that biometric passports/ID cards can be 'read' in other member states.

The UK paper does make two telling points. First, on the question of 'Privacy Enhancing Technologies' (PET), which it says, can help:

> *'in making breaches of data protection rules and violations of privacy technically more difficult.'*

But then goes on to say:

> *'However, this technology also has the potential to undermine the work of law enforcement agencies. For example, PETs may be used by individuals carrying out illegal activities on the Internet to prevent their identity being discovered.'*

Yet again the exceptional defines the norm. If some people, an unlawful minority, can exploit PETs, then this technology should be denied to all.

The second point concerns data-sharing with third countries. A regime must be in place:

> *'to share data quickly when it is in the EU's interests to do so and to avoid any detrimental impact on international relations.'*

In a reference to the EU-US High Level Group's report on data protection and data-sharing[27], it says:

> *'agreement on high-level principles of data protection might add value with countries unlikely to achieve adequacy overall, but with whom we need to share considerable law enforcement data, for example, with the USA.'*

Thus the need to 'share considerable law enforcement data ... with the USA' should not be impeded by data protection and privacy.[28]

This despite the fact that, in the words of Barry Steinhardt of the American Civil Liberties Union (ACLU), US agencies through agreements with EU service providers, which allow data and content to 'pass through' the USA, are conducting extrajudicial surveillance of Europeans and:

> *'internet transactions and email between Europeans is increasingly sent through servers in the US.*
>
> *In many ways this situation is similar to the SWIFT case: transactions between two individuals in Europe may well transit through US telecommunications companies and as a result will be made accessible to the US government.*
>
> *This activity involves no oversight or legal protections for non-US persons. As a result, the communications of European citizens are completely vulnerable to abuse.*
>
> *We believe that this situation clearly violates European legal requirements for the fair and lawful processing of personal information.'* [29]

16

The French Government submitted another paper on 'police cooperation'.[30] It suggests that Police and Customs Cooperation Centres (PCCCs) are essential in border zones and should be 'integrated into the acquis of the Union'. They could become 'centres of crisis management capable of handling events on an international scale'. In this way:

> *'they could prefigure a "European" police of the future in which, in certain border zones, police agents of different nationalities work side by side.'*

The French paper backs the *'simplication'* of regulations, when police in a member state need to 'intervene' on the territory of another. One way would be to allow:

> *'police agents ... to perform non-coercive acts on the territory of another Member State.'*

It further suggests that 'BorderTEchNet', created by Frontex, could be a 'Model' for policing activities such as:

> *'recruiting human resources ... or to manage protest demonstrations.'*

The French paper, like others, is particularly keen on 'harmonising regulations and standardising materials for security technologies'. It gives three examples:
1) Video surveillance systems where there are a 'multiplicity of systems', which should be standardised across the EU. New CCTV systems are now digital and images can be captured, stored and searched at will.
2) Internet telephony especially Skype has become widespread and:

> *'the regulatory environment today makes it very difficult for police to legally intercept criminal use of technologies of this type.'*

3) Use of unpiloted flight systems and dirigibles. It notes that:

> *'with rare exceptions, drones (unpiloted, low-flying light aircraft that remain in view of their operators) are forbidden today in the European sky.'*

However there are economic and operational reasons why *'these technologies are potentially very efficient for use in numerous security assignments.'* 'Protected wavelengths' are also needed to pilot these aircraft.

The 'blurriness' between internal and external security

It is not unusual for the EU to invent new terms such as 'interoperability' and the 'principle of availability', now there is 'blurriness' used in the context of suggesting that internal and external security are one, intrinsically interdependent.[31] Thus:

> *'the line between external security (=military) and internal security (=police) is becoming increasingly blurred.'* (5/2007/DE)

As one of the introductory documents on this theme notes:

> *'protecting the European Union's internal security involves not only measures at and within the Community borders, but also and in particular engagement abroad. This is the basic idea at the heart of the 2003 European Security Strategy, which said "in an era of globalisation, distant threats may be as much a concern as those that are near at hand ... the first defence will often be abroad".'*(5/2207/DE)

It is a logic that allows all external threats – as perceived by those in power – to be invoked to legitimate all manner of measures internally. In the EU lexicon, and in papers before the Future Group, the main 'threats' are:

> *'terrorist attacks and migration flows.'* (e.g.: 5/2007/DE)

From the perspective of the European Security and Defence Policy (ESDP) the 'causes and roots of instability and radicalisation' should be combated by, on the one hand, development aid and economic cooperation and, on the other, in those areas where 'threats' exist to:

> *'replace, rebuild or support structures in the field of public security and order following crises.'*

In addition to the military (peace-making or peace-keeping) and police there are 'civil protection teams' rebuilding government infrastructures. This approach is known as 'non-military crisis management', agreed in 2000, which is intended to rebuild a state to meet 'EU standards'.[32]

In addition to the dozens of EU Police Missions (EUPM) undertaken and continuing in Africa, the Middle East and Asia[33], this paper highlights the deployment of Integrated Police Units (IPUs). Since June 2001:

> *'the EU Police Unit responsible for planning and carrying out EU police operations has been located in the Council Secretariat.'* (5/2007/DE)

It also suggests integrating the European Gendarmerie Force (EGF) set up by Italy, Spain, France, Portugal and the Netherlands in 2005. The EGF is comprised of paramilitary police units from each state.[34] The EGF is currently outside of formal EU structure, but it is suggested that the force could be formally recognised and integrated into the ESDP as 'Integrated Police Units'. The paper notes that the role of the EGF is 'to maintain public security and order' and that it is a:

'special formation (with a strong associative component).'

'Associative' is a reference to their coercive, militarised role.

Finally, an earlier document from the German government raised the controversial issue, particularly in the UK, of deporting terrorist suspects to states with known abuses of human rights for whom there is insufficient evidence to bring them to trial:

'with regard to expulsion, deportation and surveillance of persons with a terrorist background should we launch a discussion process, between Member States and further partners, on possibilities for further cooperation or common approaches especially vis-à-vis receiving countries?'

'Further partners' can be taken to include the USA, and 'receiving countries' would include Jordan, Egypt, Algeria and Morocco.

The 'external' dimension of EU home affairs

Two of the 'thematic challenges' set out, organised crime and global migration, are familiar.[35] 'Legal certainty' for cross-border transactions raises the EU-USA Passenger Name Record scheme and:

'the difficult reconciliation of two legal systems with the potential of causing considerable economic damage to air carriers if we fail to find a solution.'

This is because especially since 11 September 2001:

'the transatlantic partnership with the US is essential for the EU.'

Differences over data protection laws should not stand in the way of the fullest cooperation:

'it is time to start thinking what we have in common rather than the differences between us.'

This is particularly so because:

'facilitated travel and investment are the backbone of our economies and a reflection of our open, democratic societies.'

Therefore:

*'consideration should be given to a **common transatlantic space** with more sharing of relevant information and at the same time more protection of personal data, expedited travel for bona fides passengers and more secure borders.'* (emphasis in original)

On data protection the EU should promote 'meaningful and enforceable data protection clauses'. However, it is recalled that the Draft Framework Decision on the transfer of personal data in police and judicial cooperation contains no EU-wide adequacy test for third states. (See Case Study on data protection below).

The paper also notes one of the consequences of the EU's planned enlargement. By 2014, Turkey's accession could be closer, leading to Iraq and Iran becoming EU 'neighbours'.

End comments

1. An 'Interim Report' from the Future Group was presented to the informal Justice and Home Affairs Council on 25-26 January 2008, under the Slovenian Council Presidency. However, this is so lacking in detail it is not of much significance.[36]

2. Four substantive areas discussed in documents submitted – the 'digital tsunami', data protection, the new 'convergence' principle, and EU-USA relations are considered in Case Studies in Chapters 5-8.

3. It is perhaps salutary to note that under the EU financial framework for 2007-2012, the allocated budget under the heading 'Security' will increase by 968% over the period.

4

Executive Summary and Final Report 'Freedom, Security and Privacy' – the area of European Home Affairs

A number of the ideas presented in Chapter 3 surface again in this Chapter as they show which were agreed in the final report.

Drawing on the full report, *Freedom, Security and Privacy: European Home Affairs,* and the background documents, it is argued that the 'Futures' programme is based on highly debatable ideological assumptions.[37] The underlying assumption is set out at the end of the executive summary, namely that citizens need to understand decisions so it is proposed that:

> *'a structured and consolidated compilation of all law instruments in force in the area of European Home Affairs should be made available to the public on the internet.'*

So, too, should the transposition of directives and framework decisions plus 'certain agreements between Member States'. These 'Codices' would make the acquis more transparent:

> *'citizens need to be able to understand on which level a decision was taken and why.'*

First, the Justice and Home Affairs Council was set up in December 1993, under the Maastricht Treaty – preceded by the Trevi Group (1976-1993) – and was followed by the Amsterdam Treaty in 1999, which is still in force. Some 800 plus measures have been adopted and put into practice yet only now, 15 years later, is the Council thinking about making this information easily accessible to the public. Since 1997, the Statewatch European Monitoring and Documentation Centre (SEMDOC) has provided exactly this service – even after a grant request to the Commission was rejected because of our critical work on access to documents, which included complaints of maladministration against the Council.[38]

Second, access to information about the Commission's work is a persistent source of complaint from practitioners (e.g.: EU information centres, lawyers, academics, civil society). When the Commission adopts a proposal a press release is issued on the day, but the document on which it is based may not become publicly available for days or even weeks later. While this allows the Commission to set the agenda in the media, it is antithetical to the democratic standard. At the national level, it would never be tolerated for a government to issue a press release but not the text of a parliamentary Bill at the same time.

Also, it often fails to monitor the adoption (transposition) of measures into national law and to make these transpositions publicly available.[39] This is compounded by the hundreds of references, in EU measures, to the fact that powers shall be exercised in accordance with 'national law' – but, if these national laws are not available, how can the legality of actions taken be assessed?

Third, the two points above demonstrate the EU institutions' failure to undertake basic tasks in a democracy, failures that would not be acceptable at national level. Instead of tackling the 'democratic deficit' by the much-vaunted notion of 'deepening democracy', there was an assumption that 'Hague' followed 'Tampere' and 'Stockholm' (presuming it is adopted under the Swedish Council Presidency in the second half of 2009) will follow 'Hague' – and that the Council (the EU governments) will have the final say while 'taking into account' (i.e.: usually ignoring) the views of national and European parliaments and civil society.

Moreover, the Commission's Report on the implementation of the Hague Programme *only* 'monitors adoption (transposition) of measures' *not* their implementation, that is, how they are put into practice.[40] Similarly there has only been one review, in 2003, by the Commission of the implementation of the 1995 EC Directive on data protection, in the 13 years since its adoption – and, despite recognised basic failings at national level, it recommended no amendments were needed.

Fourth, there is the extraordinary assumption at the conclusion of the executive summary that citizens:

'will better make their own the actions of the European Union.' (p11)

Thus, if 'they' (the people) know what is going on and how it is decided then they will embrace EU values and actions. That is to say that if 'we' (the people) understand what has gone on, and what is planned, we will inevitably agree and support EU actions – they cannot conceive of anyone being pro-Europe and not agreeing with their policies and actions. The authors of this report, as is typical of 'political élites', those who inhabit the 'Brussels bubble', fail to understand that there are many – including Statewatch since 1991 – who do know and understand what the EU has done, and what it is planning, and who fundamentally disagree with the direction it is taking in justice and home affairs.

Fifthly, what are the assumed 'shared values' of the EU? Both sides of the debate would agree that 'freedom', 'security', 'justice', 'privacy' and 'democracy' are important, but utterly disagree on the practice. For example, the EU institutions maintain that it has 'balanced' the needs of 'security' and 'civil liberties' when they have not.[41]

EU 'values' are not 'shared' or 'common' but are those of the ruling élite, who assume they can define and propagate a 'consensus' where there is none.

How the Interior Ministers were briefed

A short summary of the report – just over three pages rather than the full nine pages in the draft Executive Summary – was prepared for Ministers to consider over a 'working lunch' in Cannes on 7 July 2008.[42]

The 'challenges' for 2010 to 2014 are set out as, first:

> *'the growing link between the internal situation in the EU and the external pressures which it is facing, both in terms of security and migration.'*

Second, technological advances for information sharing. Third, to find a 'European way' to reconcile demands for privacy and:

> *'the need to use technological resources to manage immigration, control borders and combat terrorism and organised crime.'*

How are these challenges to be met? First, by information sharing, the interoperability of files and security equipment. Second, by the creation of a 'common culture' for Member States' agencies (sounds a bit like 'pooling sovereignty'). Third, the 'simplification' of laws to bring about 'closer operational cooperation' in 'criminal investigations and the management of external borders'. Fourth, 'solidarity mechanisms' for one-off operations with 'joint teams' and 'joint tools' (i.e.: security equipment).

Finally, the short paper sets out the overall philosophy. Initially, the EU focused on 'enabling' Member States 'to work together on common problems'. This was followed by making information available under the 'principle of availability' under the Hague programme.[43] Now:

> *'today, a new phase is to be launched. Following a "running-in" period, existing tools must now be used to the full, in an efficient and coordinated manner. It has been found that EU Member States often still have difficulties in communicating or setting up common action, so the principle of convergence may serve as a guideline for the European Union in the period which is now beginning. It would apply to all*

areas which could help bring Member States closer together: bringing together officers, institutions, practices, equipment and legal frameworks. It would allow a comprehensive and coherent view of the development of European Union policy on security and immigration in the future work programme.'

The Future Group report on European Home Affairs
Part 1
Introduction

'Home Affairs' policy now takes place in an increasingly 'global environment'. This climate is made up of globalisation, striking the 'right balance between mobility, security and privacy' ('mobility' refers to the movement of people, goods and information); the 'increasing 'blurriness' (that word again) of internal and external security; and the 'borderless use of information and communications technologies' linked to the need 'to protect sensitive data in an exemplary matter' – this is a reference to keeping data held by state agencies safe, perhaps in the knowledge of the catastrophic data losses in the UK.

Overarching structural challenges

Borrowing the term 'European model' from first pillar economic and social policy-making, the report says citizens expect:

'the provision of security and the safeguard of liberty and privacy by the State.'

Quite how liberty and privacy will be 'safeguarded' is never set out. We are then told that it is:

'indispensable that decision-making is transparent and comprehensible. Citizens will welcome a decision taken by "Brussels" if the responsibilities are clear and the added value is obvious.'

It goes without saying that decision-making in a democracy should be open and understandable. But decision-making in justice and home affairs is incomprehensible to all but a few experts. Even when it should become clearer, as when the European Parliament gained the power of co-decision in asylum and immigration, it became less open because of secret 'trilogue' deals between the parliament rapporteurs and the Council.[44]

Moreover, it is not at all apparent that if people could see and understand the decision-making process that they would necessarily agree with the policy to be adopted. It does not seem to have occurred to the authors that greater understanding can also lead to greater dissent.

Under the sub-heading 'Better Regulation and Simplification' there is an admission that with the plethora of measures – directives, framework decisions, decisions, recommendations, etc – adopted since 1976:

> *'it is becoming increasingly difficult and time-consuming to monitor the proper implementation of European Union Directives by as many as 27 Member States.'*

This is a embarrassed way of admitting that the Commission is failing to monitor the implementation of Justice and Home Affairs measures. If they are not monitoring 'implementation', which is simply limited to the transposition into national law, and have no mechanisms in place for monitoring the *practices* across the EU – neither by the Commission nor the European Parliament – the Ministers do not have a clue what is going on.

Nor will this be sorted out by introducing 'Codices', described as 'bundling' together EU legislation in the field.

Horizontal political challenges

First, there is preserving the 'European model ... by balancing mobility, security and privacy'. These three ideas should, the report says, be viewed as a 'triangle' (a concept taken straight from the UK paper). It argues that there is a general perception that measures to increase security such as making personal travel data available to police and others, and increased checks at airports, undermine privacy, whereas measures to increase mobility 'are seen to have an adverse effect on security'. Their conclusion is:

> *'if citizens did not feel secure, then it is highly likely they would not wish to travel at all.'*

People certainly want to feel safe when they travel, but many will need a lot of convincing that throwing away mountains of water bottles and taking off belts and shoes has much to do with safety. Equally, concern is not going to go away over the gathering of travel data from everyone in the EU which may be used for virtually any crime, and remain on record for years.

And apparently 'technological developments' and databases:

> *'can ensure more security for citizens and at the same time greater protection of their right to privacy.'*

Exactly how is not at all clear. Greater 'protection' is an ambiguous notion. Do they mean they will do their best to make sure that data is not lost or stolen? Or are they suggesting that individuals can have real control of the data held on them? Or are we meant to believe that a benevolent state will never lose or abuse our data?

Next, 'state-of-the-art information networks and databases' are needed, as are 'information technology management strategies' that support 'political objectives'. This, in turn, means that there has to be a 'common European standard' for 'data storage and transmission ... and harmonised technical data formats.' Thus, throughout the European state the technology used at the national level has to be harmonised, and plump contracts awarded to the successful multinationals.[45]

Part II
'Preserving Internal Security and External Stability'

Under this concept there are both refinements of existing developments and new proposals. Its starts with police cooperation where 'law enforcement cooperation' should be 'deepened' and the national agencies should get 'closer to each other'. Moreover, the 'environment' of police cooperation should be enhanced by 'integrating police file management and security technologies'. That is, there should be 'convergence' of training, best practices, standardised equipment to ensure interoperability, and technological abilities including:

'video surveillance, internet telephony and police use of unpiloted aircraft'

plus collective licensing costs of agreed equipment, computer and translation programmes. For example, under the so-called 'Swedish' Framework Decision on information sharing, this could be fulfilled by:

*'means of creating **automated** data transfer instruments.'* (emphasis added)

The creation of Police and Customs Cooperation Centres (PCCC) both in 'border zones' and as centres:

'of crisis management capable of handling events on an international scale.'

Meanwhile, cross-border criminal investigations are said to require the 'simplification of regulations' by eliminating the need for judicial authorisation. It uses the example of requests for 'non-coercive acts' being carried out for another Member State based on simple 'written requests' agency to agency. 'Non-coercive' could cover a number of 'sins'. In the UK it is coercive to put a 'bug' in a room but not to record conversations from outside of a building or in a public place. Nor would it be 'coercive' to gather intelligence on banking, work and friendship networks.

In the 'fight against terrorism' it is suggested that, 'best practices' should be promoted with third states:

'concerning the legal tools for expulsion and surveillance.'

When the EU calls for measures to tackle terrorism this is nearly always justified by saying that 'law enforcement agencies' (LEAs, police, immigration and customs) need new powers. Traditionally, the security services (internal) and intelligence agencies (external) are rarely mentioned, even though they, not the LEAs, are at the forefront of tackling al-Qaeda-style terrorism. Here the Future Report treads cautiously, 'careful consideration' should be given to the question of:

'whether, and to what extent, European union structures could contribute to bringing these divergent interests in line with each other.'

This is because the much-vaunted 'principle of availability' runs up against the 'principle of confidentiality' when discussing exchanges of information between the security and intelligence agencies. Cooperation on specific cases can and does happen, but intelligence sharing in general does not. Among the obstacles is the special relationship between the USA and the UK, in place since the UKUSA agreement of 1947.[46]

It is also recommended that the role of Financial Intelligence Units (FIUs) should be enhanced with:

'the systematic monitoring of financial transactions in the Union'

and the power of LEAs extended to:

'authorise them to use databases such as SWIFT.' [47]

In order to 'Preserve External Stability' in 'third countries' there is a need for greater coordination between 'military, police, civil protection, development aid and rule of law devices', including the:

'integration of the "European Gendarmerie Force" and civilian police units from Member States into the legal framework of the EU.'

The EGF is comprised of paramilitary police units from Spain, France, Italy, Netherlands and Portugal.[48]

Finally:

'the Group considers close and continuous cooperation with the United States to be indispensable'

and in the medium term:

'this cooperation should lead to greater convergence, including the different legal frameworks of data protection'

and:

'by 2014, the European Union should also make up its mind with regard to the political objective of achieving a Euro-Atlantic area of cooperation with the USA in the field of Freedom, Security and Justice.'

This ia another example of 'convergence', this time between the EU and the USA, across the *whole* field of justice and home affairs (See Chapter 8).

Part III
Managing migration, asylum, external borders and integration

Many of the objectives in this Chapter may be familiar as they have been started, or discussed:

'easing the negative repercussions of demographic ageing'

is to be met by 'legal migration'. While, at the same time, 'illegal employment' of those who manage to enter the EU – maybe even years or generations ago – is to be stamped out, and enforced by a coordinated European return policy. In July 2008, the EU adopted the 'outrageous' Returns Directive, which was not only opposed by hundreds of civil society groups and the Council of Europe, but was also condemned as hypocritical by leaders from Central and Latin America and Africa.[49]

The hypocrisy of these policies is well illustrated by the report contention that the:

'overall aim must be to ensure that people migrate out of choice rather than necessity.'

When the West (USA and EU) stops exploiting third world resources and markets many people will not have to flee from poverty or to search for work and, when they stop supporting pro-Western authoritarian regimes, many fewer will have to flee from persecution.

The report talks quite unrealistically of 'dialogue', 'cooperation' and 'partnership' with countries of origin and transit when it is usually a one-way set of demands on the third world.[50]

The Hague Programme ideology was 'carrot and stick', making aid dependent on cooperation over taking people back (e.g.: re-admission agreements).[51] Now the:

> *'Group strongly advocates developing a holistic concept covering: e.g.: development, migration, security, economic, financial, trade and foreign policy aspects.'*

This pincer-like approach could, in time, be complimented by EU-USA's 'convergence' of interests and aims, too.

Asylum policy

There is a frank admission that existing minimum standards:

> *'which leave Member States a wide margin of discretion in their application, have not led to a level playing field and do not guarantee equality of protection across the EU.'*

So after an evaluation there will be further harmonisation.

'Regional Protection Programmes' (RPP), after evaluation, should be developed or redesigned and a 'Common resettlement instrument' created.

Modernising the Schengen border and visa approach

A 'state-of-the-art border control system' is to be accompanied by an 'awareness' campaign promoting 'the advantages of increased use of information and communication technologies'.

The 'E-Border' concept for checks and controls, in the integrated Border Management Strategy, needs the following:

– a registered travellers programme, i.e. pre-registering with 'iris scans' and fingerprints to allow speedy clearance;

– an Electronic System for Travel Authorisation (ESTA), following on exactly from the US model. Permission to travel (watch-list checks) has to be given before buying a ticket. This is presumably for travel into the EU. Although it should be noted that the planned EU-PNR system may end up recording the travel of everyone in and out of the EU, within the EU and within each country by air, land and sea;

– an exit/entry system for third country nationals;

– 'automated border control systems for European Union nationals', with the spin that this will 'speed up passenger flows';

In addition, for 'smoother' border control, the European Border

Surveillance System (Eurosur) should be developed.

While, to make border checks as efficient and 'customer-friendly' as possible, there should be the merging of border and customs controls and:

'a one-stop approach integrating all checks and controls carried out for different purposes, i.e. relating to persons, goods, veterinary and phyto-sanitary, pollution, terrorism and organised crime.'

Note that examples are given for the 'different purposes', so the 'purposes' could include all crime however minor, and/or public order 'suspects'.

Common Visa Application Centres in third countries should be stepped up and 'uniform European Schengen visas should be issued'.

Further developing Frontex

There are, the report says, 'widely differing views on how far European agencies should be strengthened'. But there are 'several far-reaching measures' that are recommended:

– Frontex agency missions are apparently 'undermined by the lack of precise legal provisions', which, in layperson's terms, includes the need to further re-write the international law of the sea so that they can stop, search and turn back vessels in the Mediterranean and off the West African coast;

– 'Frontex Reinforcement Teams' should be 'speedily' implemented involving the secondment of Member States' border policing experts;

– Frontex should be 'closely involved with the European Surveillance System';[52]

– Regional and/or specialised branches should be established;

– there should be a 'Frontex tool box', proven security and surveillance equipment;

– Frontex needs to be given responsibility to:

'initiate, organise and coordinate joints operations'

as well as:

'return flights to third countries'

which would presumably mean that the IOM (International Organisation on Migration) would lose this role.[53]

– Frontex needs to be given the power to regularly 'evaluate and inspect' national border forces, replacing the 'very infrequent'

30

Schengen evaluations;
– there should be joint 'calls for tender' and 'further coordinating options in the field of procurement'. As in the policing field, there should be 'convergence' of equipment and technology leading to 'synergies', cost savings and 'better interoperability'. This in turn will help generate:

'a common border police "corporate identity".'

Enhancing cooperation with third states

The emphasis here is to try and enlist the active cooperation of the third states that are seen as the source of 'problems' for the EU, for example, for 'illegal immigration to be curbed at its roots'. With this in mind, the idea is to be much more interventionist, not just at EU borders and at the negotiating table, but in these countries themselves: offers of easier visas for the middle classes of the third world and finance to bring in EU-style border controls, checks and documents. Frontex should take the lead in the target countries to convey EU 'strategies' and to 'advise' on producing and issuing forgery-proof documents.

As to Frontex sea patrols, for example in the Mediterranean, the reports wants its remit to be extended to:

'include the territorial waters and "search and rescue areas" of third countries affected'

and agreements, negotiated by Frontex, for joint patrols. In parallel:

'joint return measures should be facilitated.'

It is not at all clear that North African states will agree to the EU patrolling its territorial waters or to accepting, without question, the deportation of people the EU says are 'illegal'. Indeed, the reaction of African states, including Libya, to the EU Returns Directive agreed in July was very hostile.[54]

Part IV
Developing civil protection

This is described as the need to protect people, property and the environment where one or more member states are affected. European 'added value' means putting together resources and establishing a 'tool box', creating a 'dynamic platform' for the Common European and Coordination Information System (CECIS), and developing the Monitoring and Information Centre (MIC).

Part V
Using new technologies and information networks

The power of 'new technologies' peppers the Future Group Report. In addition to law enforcement and security, it is in 'border management' where the 'integrated control of EU borders, up and down stream' is recommended. Under 'civil protection' improved information management is called for, with 'better interoperability of operational techniques'.

Overall, it is argued that in the 'digital tsunami environment' (an insensitive phrase, to say the least) citizens' expectations of 'proactive protection' become 'ever more acute', especially as traditional measures to protect privacy 'will become less and less effective', thus:

> *'"privacy enhancing technologies" are absolutely essential to guarantee civil and political rights in the age of cyberspace.'*

The document is silent on how this should be done.

The Report's main emphasis is, almost exclusively, on the opportunities the 'digital tsunami' gives public security organisations to:

> *'have access to almost limitless amounts of potentially useful information.'*

For 'public security organisations' to 'master this data tsunami' will require 'automated data analysis', and getting this through to a 'multitude of stakeholders' in the agencies across the EU. 'Interoperability' is assumed (being able to access databases across the EU), what is needed is a:

> *'platform approach to delivering public security.'*

This service oriented approach means that:

> *'outputs from different parts of the system can be shared (within and across organisations), and to build **converged** platforms ... move to converged networks (or where necessary solutions that ensure all their networks can "talk" to each other), and ... ensure all data streams are digital and capable of being meshed together.'*
> (emphasis added)

This sounds like meaningless business-style 'gobbledegook' (nonsense), but it is not. It represents a mega-shift in the power of the state and its agencies (see also Case Study below). For example, the 'principle of availability' means that on a 'case-by-case' basis, through 'interoperable' systems, data and intelligence can be gathered by an agency in one state from a number of other EU states. However, the report argues that:

> 'this is an opportune moment to go beyond the limited perspective of a case-by-case approach and aim for a holistic objective in law enforcement information management.'

In contrast to an 'uncoordinated and incoherent palette of information systems', there would be a:

> 'European Union Law Enforcement Information Management Strategy (EU IMS) ... aiming at a professional, business-oriented and cost-effective use of information technology and information networks.'

The logic of the EU IMS would do away with national crime and intelligence systems and, under the 'convergence principle', bring in standardised IT equipment (bulk purchased and licensed) linked to EU-wide networks/platforms. Necessary preparatory elements for this strategy are the automated transfer of data and intelligence, and defining:

> 'what types of information are useful, needed or required ... So far a total of 49 types of relevant information have been identified, of which six have been the subject of an assessment as to how the principle of availability could be applied to them.'

These are, as set out in the Prüm Decision:

> 'DNA, fingerprints, ballistics, vehicle registration, telephone numbers and minimum data for identification of persons contained in civil registers.'

The report recommends that 'a top ten list of data categories ... should be identified'.

At the end of this section it is argued that 'data protection' is 'essential' for the implementation of the 'principle of availability'. In addition to the 'Framework Decision on data protection' – which will govern the transfer of data between EU member states and is utterly useless – 'additional standards ... might be needed.'[55]

'Effort', too, should be directed to 'adapting' national data protection laws and practices to meet:

> 'current law enforcement realities.'

The last paragraph says that 'greater public understanding of the benefits of data sharing between Member States should be a priority'. Citizens need to have it made clear to them:

'how information will be processed and protected, on the basis of proportionality and necessity.'

The 'necessity' of the state to gather, process, further process, and act on accumulated personal data/intelligence is assumed to be proportional to the purpose for which it is gathered – for if the 'purpose' of gathering the data/intelligence on everyone in the EU is to 'protect' us all from 'threats', as defined by the EU, then it is clearly proportional.

This description of the use of IT and technology in the Future Group's vision for 'European Home Affairs', as set out in their report, may be difficult to comprehend, but all will become clear in the Case Study below.

Part VI
Implementing the external dimension
of Home Affairs policy

Again, the need for Foreign/External Affairs, Development Policy, Defence and Home Affairs to take an integrated approach is emphasised. This means that all 'leverages' (blackmail, pressure, 'carrot and stick') can be brought to bear on third world states.

'Action Oriented Papers' are to be drawn up, and then an 'issues paper', followed by identifying 'which third countries are of vital interest for cooperation'.

The greater use of technologies and databases in the EU (e.g.: SIS II, Visa Information System, and an exit-entry system) is going to involve:

'increased data exchanges with third countries. A clear legal framework for protection of data inside the EU and when transferred to third countries is essential.'

How this is to be achieved is not set out, just the general assertion that the EU has a 'strong political interest' by signalling to third countries:

'that data transfer can take place provided that certain guarantees are in place.'

'Guarantees' are not spelt out and are not the same as the required 'adequacy' test to meet EU standards as set out in law.

The US is the subject of special attention. The EU and the USA should:

'cooperate bilaterally in order to secure visa-free travel for all Member States.'

At present 15 EU Member States, including Slovenia but not Greece, are part of the US Visa Waiver Programme – 12 Member States are not. The EU has been trying to get all 27 states into the scheme for nearly two years, but every time an agreement seems to be imminent the US side changes its laws and hence its demands.[56] When the EU tried to insist all Member States be treated equally, the US simply went behind the EU's back and negotiated bilaterally with seven EU countries (See Chapter 8).

Visa-free travel will become a complete misnomer when the US introduces its Electronic System for Travel Authorisation (ESTA). Anyone intending to travel to the USA will have to apply in advance of their departure for permission to travel, their application having been thoroughly vetted against watch-lists.

The EU intends to introduce its own ESTA and exit-entry system for all third country nationals including the USA. However, mindful of wanting to become a global player in alliance with the USA, this report says the EU and USA:

'should cooperate in relevant international fora in order to create an environment where travel is safe, secure and expeditious for bona fide travellers.'

This is code for saying a joint EU-USA system for the control and surveillance of travel will set a global norm – and profit for their multinationals.

At present the EU and USA cooperate on terrorism, border security, international crime, cyber-crime, drug trafficking and trafficking of people, and 'binding agreement' on data protection is needed. It ends by saying that:

'consideration could be further given to a common transatlantic space with more sharing of relevant information.'

Conclusion

As in the Tampere and Hague programmes, some of the proposals are explicit while others are only alluded to in very general terms. While some new directions are clearly based on papers submitted to the group, others need further explanation and investigation. Four Case Studies below are intended to flesh-out where the EU is going.

5

Case Study
The 'digital tsunami' and the EU surveillance state

The Future Group proposes to harness the 'digital tsunami' by European (and national) agencies predicating state surveillance over a very wide range of human activity.

Two of the Future Group's documents are considered here:
1) sections from the final report: 'Freedom, Security and Privacy – the area of European Home Affairs' (referred to as the 'final report') and
2) a 'concept' paper from the Portuguese Council Presidency entitled: 'Public security, privacy and technology in Europe: Moving Forward: Concept paper on the European strategy to transform public security organisations in a connected world' (referred to as the 'paper')[57]. As we shall see, the obscure language used in the former is firmly embedded in the latter.

Using new technologies and information networks

The final report argues that in the 'digital tsunami environment' citizens' expectations of 'proactive protection' become 'ever more acute', especially as traditional measures to protect privacy 'will become less and less effective', thus:

> 'privacy-enhancing technologies are absolutely essential to guarantee civil and political rights in the age of cyberspace.'

The document is silent on how this should be done. The main emphasis is, almost exclusively, on the opportunities the 'digital tsunami' gives 'public security organisations' to:

> 'have access to almost limitless amounts of potentially useful information.'

For 'public security organisations' to 'master this data tsunami' will require 'automated data analysis' to get this through to a 'multitude of stakeholders' in the agencies across the EU. 'Interoperability' is assumed (being able to access databases across the EU), but what is needed is a:

> 'platform approach to delivering public security.'

A 'service oriented' approach means that:

> 'outputs from different parts of the system can be shared (within and across

36

*organisations) and to build **converged** platforms ... move to converged networks (or where necessary solutions that ensure all their networks can "talk" to each other) and ... ensure all data streams are digital and capable of being meshed together.'* (emphasis added)

For example, the 'principle of availability' means that on a 'case-by-case' basis, through 'interoperable' systems, data and intelligence can be gathered by an agency in one state from a number of other EU states. However, remember the report argued that:

'this is an opportune moment to go beyond the limited perspective of a case-by-case approach and aim for a holistic objective in law enforcement information management.'

In contrast to an 'uncoordinated and incoherent palette of information systems', there would be a:

'European Union Law Enforcement Information Management Strategy (EU IMS) ... aiming at a professional, business-oriented and cost-effective use of information technology and information networks.'

The EU 'surveillance state'

At its meeting in October 2007, the Future Group was presented with a 'concept' paper from the Portuguese Council Presidency. It spells out in detail the thinking and intent underneath the obscure language in the full report's section on: 'Using new technologies and information networks'. The 'concept paper' opens with the statement that:

'technology is not neutral: it must be put at the service of security with respect for the way of life of the citizen in democratic countries and can have a decisive contribution towards making a global world more secure.'

This statement begs the question of exactly how, if technology is 'put at the service of security', it can, at the same time, have 'respect' for the way of life of citizens. Surely, technology should 'serve' the people and 'serve' security only in so far as it does not undermine individual and fundamental rights. This paper, however, assumes the former to reflect the consensus of governments in the EU; 'public security' comes first. It can be argued that it is not 'public security' the public want, but rather 'public safety'. Indeed, if a concept of 'public safety', based on people's needs, were used instead of 'public security', based on the state's needs, a whole different set of policies and practices might emerge.

The paper draws attention to the:

'development and integration of satellite and airborne monitoring capabilities, the use of GMES technologies including multi-layer mapping with modelling tools and the development of shared, interactive and secure information, communication and analysis tools.'

GMES, Global Monitoring for Environment and Security, is an EU initiative for the implementation of information services dealing with the environment and security. It uses 'observation data' from 'Earth Observation' satellites and ground based information, which integrates and makes accessible data from multiple sources. This allows public and private actors to 'anticipate, intervene and control'.

The next section in the Portuguese Council Presidency paper is *'The digital tsunami and its consequences for public security organisations'*. As more and more 'people, machines and environments are connected', this vastly increases the amount of:

'potential information for use in the day-to-day operations of public security organisations.

One obvious illustration is the ability to track the location of any active mobile phone (and to know where it was last switched off and last switched on). This is just the beginning. In the next few years billions of items in the physical world will be connected, using technologies such as radio-frequency identification (RFID), broadband wireless (WiFi, WiMAX), satellite and wireless (Bluetooth, wireless USB, ZigBee). This means it will be possible to trace more and more objects in real-time and to analyse their movement and activity retrospectively ... In the near future most objects will generate streams of digital data about their location and use – revealing patterns and social behaviours which public security professionals can use to prevent or investigate incidents.'

The 'objects' referred to also include people who could be tracked through their car, mobile phone or the clothes they are wearing.

The paper goes on to look at digital transactions, use of biometrics and online behaviour:

'all credit or debit-related purchases already generate monitorable and searchable real-time information; but more and more transactions will be of this kind as we move towards a cashless society ...

These trends will be reinforced as biometric measurements are used to enhance security at more and more locations – whether public places such as town halls or train stations; private locations such as amusement venues; or places of work.'

This assumes the widespread use of peoples' biometrics (fingerprints, facial scans or iris scans) in everyday life, once they have been collected by national EU states for passports and ID cards.[58]

'Most large cities have already seen a significant increase in the use of closed circuit

38

television (CCTV), and usage (by public and private sector organisations) is likely to increase further and to shift from the current analogue technologies to more easily storable and searchable digital technologies.

Further accelerating the tsunami of data is online behaviour. Social networks such as MySpace, Facebook and Second Life – and indeed all forms of online activity – generate huge amounts of information that can be of use to public security organisations.'

Next generation 'searchable digital' videos of public and private places suggests lifetime databanks, with the ability to conduct historical searches based on a person's image.[59]

The paper suggests that the capacity now exists, or will very soon, where the state will be able to combine data from different sources on every individual – financial transactions, train journeys, visits to a town hall, a fairground, images from 'searchable digital technologies', internet usage and social habits together with state records, citizen registration, National Insurance details, schools, universities, criminal records, tax record, health record, driving licence and motoring offences, insurance details and more which could be used to monitor and control social, economic and political life. If this seems an extreme view just read what the Portuguese Council Presidency goes on to say:

'These trends have huge implications for public security. Citizens already leave many digital traces as they move around. What is clear, however, is that the number of those traces (and the detailed information they contain) is likely to increase by several orders of magnitude in the next ten years.

Every object the individual uses, every transaction they make and almost everywhere they go, will create a detailed digital record. This will generate a wealth of information for public security organisations, and create huge opportunities for more effective and productive public security efforts.'

Is 'privacy enhancing technology' a non-starter?

The final report mentioned that 'Privacy enhancing technologies' were essential if people were to be convinced of the need for this development. Here in this background paper, however, this is recognised but is also fatally undermined. The paper says that fundamental privacy issues are raised on 'how much information about the behaviour of citizens should be shared'. There is no reference to terrorism or even crime, but simply 'information about the *behaviour* of citizens' being hoovered up. It then goes on to say:

'paradoxically, those same tools can also be used by terrorists and other criminals. Thus, if data are automatically anonymised after a certain lapse of time, that

procedure may erase evidence of crimes; encryption tools prevent hacking when information is transmitted over the internet and protect personal data against unlawful processing, but may also help conceal criminal plans; cookie-cutters enhance compliance with the principle that data must be processed fairly and that the data subject must be informed about the processing going on, but may also make ineffective police efforts to gather information on illegal activities.'

Indeed, when it comes to 'balancing' the first need against the second it is 'security' that has always won since 11 September 2001. Just look at the draft Framework Decision on data protection on police and judicial cooperation – covering the exchange of data/intelligence between member states and outside the EU about to be adopted by the Council. The Commission proposal was thrown out and rewritten by law enforcement officers and officials, who ignored all the proposals by EU data protection bodies for meaningful privacy provisions.[60]

Three 'Challenges'

The Portuguese paper says that there are three 'Challenges', the first of which, presented under the heading 'Automate and master data analysis', is that the 'digital tsunami':

'data monitoring and analysis will become much more automated.'

Drawing on the practice of financial traders, brokers and credit card companies, who use sophisticated programmes to analyse changes and trends, the paper says that:

*'**machines** are able not just to analyse records of transactions, but also to analyse visual information as well. Current systems can already identify individuals by their gait or flag up particular types of image, e.g.: unattended luggage or a person lying on the ground, apparently injured. Next generation systems are likely to be able to watch for, find and follow even more tightly defined objects, behaviour patterns or events.*

These developments mean routine data monitoring and analysis will increasingly be handled by machines; the system will then flag up exceptions (unusual behaviour and anomalies) for human investigation. Some law enforcement agencies are already familiar with this approach in their suspicious transaction monitoring activities, carried out by specialised agencies tasked with anti-money laundering activity. But this approach will need to be much more widely understood.' (emphasis added)

When put together, 'automated monitoring and analysis' with 'machines' determining unusual or unacceptable behaviour, the next step is easy; you get 'machine' driven responses. Thus, 'networked systems' will not just monitor live situations but the 'machine':

'will start to respond to it intelligently.'

So now we have 'intelligent' machines. Moreover, the systems or 'machines' will:

'work across multiple data streams and multiple types of data stream. For example, if someone in an airport starts making a series of unusual mobile phone calls, the system might monitor the video streams of the areas where that person is more sensitively than it would normally. Or, it might check passenger travel information to see if that person or someone related to them is due to arrive or depart in the next couple of hours.'

Who, or rather what (if it is a machine), will determine if a mobile phone call is 'unusual'? What if you are doing your neighbour a favour by picking up their grandparents from the airport – you are not related to them and are a bit anxious that you will not recognise them?

The second 'challenge' is 'making decision-making more distributed', which is making sure that everyone in the chain of public security organisations can get instant and real-time information.

The third 'challenge' is to 'transform decision support'. Employing 'Mashups' ('web applications that combine data from two or more sources into a 'single tool') means that:

'in the near future public security organisations will be building portals that aggregate a huge range of data sources into personalized cockpits for different decision-makers'

which, in turn, means that:

'IT systems will increasingly have automated policies that perform actions on decisions and/or destinations.'

It is not hard to imagine a scenario where a person is picked up by CCTV running in a tube station: is this person running because they have attacked someone, running away from an attacker, or just running for the train?

Echoing the final report the Council Presidency paper says that EU member states 'individually and collectively' should take a 'platform' approach to 'delivering public security'. They need, it says, to move beyond interoperability to a 'services-oriented approach' and 'converged platforms' so that all the networks can 'talk' to each other'.

After all, in an increasingly connected world:

'public security organisations will have access to almost limitless amounts of potentially useful information.'

Conclusion

This paper, and the final report, were drawn up by high-level officials and agreed by EU Ministers. They, frighteningly, really do believe they have and are 'balancing' the demands of security and civil liberties; they embrace the new technology – if it is technologically possible why should it not be used; they assume that the 'digital tsunami' should be harvested by public security organisations simply because it is there; and assume, too, that everyone accepts that the 'threats' they proclaim require such a gargantuan and undiscussed leap. There is no recognition that people not only want to live and travel in safety, but also want protection from the activities of an all-mighty state.

The creation of a surveillance state, for that is what is being proposed, will take the EU further down the road to authoritarianism, a path which looks less and less likely to be reversible.

In the aftermath of 11 September 2001, and for the next three or four years, the rationale for new powers, databases and agencies in and across the EU were presented as if they were 'exceptional' initiatives needed to meet the terrorist threat. We now know that what was termed 'exceptional' is the norm, that what were unthinkable (and politically unacceptable) uses of technology, just seven years ago, are almost upon us.

6

Case Study
The 'convergence principle'

The executive summary of the Future Group report says that the 'convergence principle':

'would apply to all areas where closer relations between Member States are possible: agents, institutions, practices, equipment and legal frameworks.'

This a sweeping proposal, but a logical development in the construction of the European state. At a stroke 'national sovereignty is pooled'. Agencies will still work at the national level but their environment will be determined (harmonised) by EU standards, and more and more roles will be undertaken at the EU level.

The 'convergence principle' underlies many of the new directions. The 'blurriness' between internal and external security means that they are in fact one. This, logically, leads to common 'threats' of terrorism and migration to legitimise all manner of initiatives. Concepts such as 'the European model' and 'tool pools' give precedence to top down decision-making to be followed at national level. The opportunities for the EU to become a global 'frontrunner' if it can harness and market new information and communications technologies is a cornerstone requiring, as a first step, 'a common European standard for data storage and transmission'. New Police Customs Cooperation Centres (PCCCs), the merging of border and customs checks, and major new roles for Frontex all point in the same direction. As do the 'needs' of third country missions where military, paramilitary, police, civil protection and 'institution-building' mechanisms should be brought together in 'Mission Situation Centres'. While the 'close and continuous cooperation with the USA ... should lead to greater convergence.'

Nor should it be forgotten that, under the Constitution-Treaty, a new Committee on Internal Security (COSI) will be set up with overall operational control throughout the EU.[61]

The 'convergence principle' follows on from the 'principle of availability' (Hague programme) of all data, information and intelligence held by all agencies across the EU and outside, to all other agencies, and the 'interoperability' of EU information systems must be

43

compatible so that all agencies can access each other's data – and this is to be complimented by **automated** access without any checks or authorisation required.

'Convergence' means not just access to data and so on, but extends to law enforcement agencies training, standards and equipment, plus a major growth in cross-border EU operations backed by a plethora of EU agencies. The 'added value', their argument goes, is:

> *'the closer Member States cooperate with each other, the clearer the shared values ... will be. The European Union will thus fulfil the desires of the peoples of Europe: they all wish to enter tomorrow's world while keeping their identity.'*[62]

It will be remembered that the Future report referred to the automated transfer of data and intelligence and the need to define:

> *'what types of information are useful, needed or required ... So far a total of 49 types of relevant information have been identified, of which six have been the subject of an assessment as to how the principle of availability could be applied to them.'*

'Convergence' is applied not only to technology and equipment, training and standards, and access to all data held by state agencies in the EU, but also to ensuring that national laws 'converge' too. In this sense 'convergence' does not mean 'harmonisation' with broad standards being set at EU level, and leaving room for national legal differences; rather, it means coming together, being the same. A good example is raised in a paper from Sweden, submitted during the Future Group discussions, which is particularly concerned with making the 'principle of availability' (POA) apply across the board.[63] The first step to implementing POA was taken on 18 December 2006:

> *'representing the classic "police-to-police" approach, i.e. indirect access to information on request.'*[64]

When combined with the use of information technology, this raised the question of whether the indirect approach above could be replaced by direct access. This question was directly related to the Prüm Treaty and the subsequent decision to adopt an EU-wide Council decision on cross-border cooperation.[65] This Council decision allows for automated access to three categories of data:
– DNA
– fingerprints
– national vehicle registration details.

The three sets of data were taken from six recommended by a

Friends of the Presidency report in 2005, which were:
- DNA
- fingerprints
- ballistics
- vehicle registration
- communications data
- data identifying person contained in civil registers.[66]

What has come back onto the agenda now – as raised in the Swedish paper – is the full set of **49 sets of data** identified in the Friends of the Presidency report. The Future report says that there is a 'data field by data field' extension of the principle of availability and that, so far, 'six have been the subject of assessment' – the six sets above (para 151). The report proposes that:

'a top ten list of data categories ... should be identified.'

Questions arise about what problems would this present? And, which additional four data sets will be included in the immediate future from the 43 sets not included?

In answer to the first, it should be recalled that the Future Group refers to existing police cooperation procedures, that is, national laws, being 'extremely constraining', and that they should be 'more flexible' (para 45). This is a coded reference to national laws which set out procedures both for the gathering of information and/or intelligence, and then for its use or transfer – which, in a number of member states, requires judicial authorisation. If the objective under the principle of availability is to allow for unregulated, automated access by agencies across the EU, legal impediments such as judicial authorisation have to be removed in the interests of 'interoperability' and 'convergence'.

The answer to the second question lies in the answers from 25 member states (plus Norway and Iceland) to a questionnaire sent out in connection with the Friends of the Presidency report from February 2005 – which is still not publicly available.[67]

Access is sought to the 49 data sets, both for the 'pre-investigation' and 'investigation stages' (a distinction that does not exist in all states, e.g. UK and Ireland). In broad terms this refers to investigation *prior* to arrest and investigation *after* arrest.

In answer to general questions about exchanging data with other EU police, 10 states said they could only access data in their

45

possession with judicial authority, and 7 states said they needed judicial authority to gather by coercive means information not in their possession.

This list of 49 data sets includes the six categories above, plus:
– other registers that describe crimes
– reports (complaints) on crimes committed
– information held by prison authorities concerning inmates
– transport companies' passenger and freight lists
– income and wealth information
– registered debts such as taxes, fines, etc
– observations or observation reports
– photographs
– film or video recordings
– questioning or other records of conversation
– statements provided by under-cover agents
– appraisals or non-appraisal information on criminal activities
– operational analyses
– documented questioning of suspects, witnesses, experts, etc
– documentation of search of premises including communications data
– documentation of telephone tapping (including so-called surplus information)
– documentation of room bugging.

Two observations might be made. First, this list of 49 data sets is not exhaustive and could be extended in the future. Second, 'convergence' giving automated access to six, 10, 49 or more sets of data requires the standardisation of equipment and programmes (interoperability) in order to work.

It should also be noted that reference is nearly always made to accessing or transferring 'information' which covers both hard factual data (e.g. arrest, charge, conviction, sentence) and 'intelligence' – which may be 'hard', based on a trusted source, or 'soft', based on an unknown or unreliable source. Nowhere is there a discussion on limiting information to that which is reliable.

How is access to be monitored in relation to the 'handling codes' for intelligence used by Europol (and most other police forces)?[68] What if the source of the information is classified as either:

'source from whom information received has in most instances proved to be unreliable' (1.C,) or *' the reliability of the source cannot be assessed' (1.D)*

and/or the 'reliability' is evaluated as:

'information which is not known personally to the source and cannot be corroborated.' (2.4)

Can this data be exchanged?

The Sweden paper also refers to an obscure *ad hoc* study carried out by the Council in 2003, compiling an inventory of third pillar information systems.[69] The Council study found that, at a time when there were 13 member states with the right of access to the Schengen Information System (SIS), there were:

'125,000 access points!!!' (exclamation marks in original)

There are now 22 Schengen member states in the EU.[70] In addition, the new SIS II system will allow access by all agencies to all the data held – under the existing SIS, data can only be accessed by agencies in the same field, i.e. police agencies can access data where they have contributed.

How many access points throughout the EU there are now, or will be soon, is a matter of guessing. Moreover, it is well known that the greater the points of access, the greater the number of people who have access, the greater the chance that data will be misplaced, lost or illegally accessed.

7

Case Study
Privacy and data protection

The report refers to privacy and data protection on many occasions and 'Privacy' is in the report's title, but it is hard to see how privacy will be protected in practice. The final report of the Future Group says citizens expect:

'the provision of security and the safeguard of liberty and privacy by the State'

and that:

'"privacy enhancing technologies" are absolutely essential to guarantee civil and political rights in the age of cyberspace.'

And the report proposes that a 'European model' be found, but it does not set out how this is to be done. Moreover, the report makes no reference to the clear reservations, if not opposition, of the agencies and officials to 'privacy enhancing technologies', expressed to the Group by the Portuguese Council Presidency and the UK, as this could be used by criminals as well as everyone else.

One is left with the impression that 'data protection' in the EU seems increasingly referred to as meaning 'protecting' the data held on people from theft or loss (as in the UK), rather than positive rights for the individual to know what is held on them and by who, to whom it has been passed, whether it has been further processed (data or intelligence added to it by a third agency), or whether it has been passed outside the EU, and to whom and why.

The concept of 'privacy', on the other hand, should mean that most of the private life of an individual is invisible to the state, and that it gathers no more information on the individual than is absolutely necessary. What information it does gather (or require) should be for a specific purpose and should not be used for another purpose (as set out in the EC 1995 Directive). Through 'data protection' laws the individual should be able to find out what information is held on them, and be told when it has been passed on to a third party, and for what purpose, as well as having the right to correct wrong information.

This definition of 'privacy' had some currency in the past but today is virtually meaningless, and will be all the more so when the 'digital tsunami' is harnessed by state agencies. Thus, 'privacy' and 'data protection' are irreconcilable with the 'principle of availability', especially when it is planned to introduce unregulated 'automated access'. So, to unravel what is likely to happen, it is necessary to look at the current situation, and what is already in the pipeline.

Data protection in the 'first pillar' (economic and social affairs) is governed by the 1995 EC Directive, which was transposed into national law by 1998. There has only been one review by the Commission of how it is working, and that was in 2003.

The 'data security' aspects are taken relatively seriously by governments and business, as losses and theft of personal data undermine credibility and trust. However, the right of the individual is another matter. In most instances transactions with multinationals such as banks, credit cards, insurance and savings schemes have a page of small print to tell you they can pass the information they hold on you where required by national law (whether inside the EU or outside) and to other branches of their conglomerates.

The 1995 Directive on data protection

The only review of its implementation was published by the European Commission in 2003, five years after implementation. In the middle of the report there are some sobering findings. The Commission reported that on personal data processing it was:

> *'hard to obtain accurate or complete information about its compliance with the law.'*

But anecdotal evidence and hard information, it says, suggested three interrelated problems:

> – *'under-resourced enforcement ... and enforcement actions have a rather low priority'* because of the wide range of tasks given to data protection supervisory authorities.
> – *'very patchy compliance by data controllers'* because *'the risks of getting caught seem low'*
> – an *'apparently low level of knowledge about their rights among data subjects.'*

The Commission's report concluded that, if confirmed, these findings *'are reasons for serious concern'*. There has been no follow-up to this report and certainly there have been no proposals to improve the working of the 1995 Directive.

A major problem with the EC Directive, which governs all financial and commercial transactions, is that businesses are using a 'template' agreed with data protection authorities back in 1998. These allow personal data to be passed on to a third party within a member state, between member states and to third states outside the EU where national laws require it. However, national laws have changed enormously between 1998 and 2008, with greater and greater powers being adopted to allow the passing of data to state agencies, with few, if any, additional safeguards or checks being put in place.

Data protection in police and judicial matters

Data protection and police and judicial matters are laid down in laws at 'national level'. However, no survey or review has ever been carried out by the Commission or any other body as to the rights and protections, or limitations, that exist from state to state under 'national laws'.

The best evidence we have of what the EU means by data protection is the draft Framework Decision on data protection in police and judicial matters. This covers the transfer of personal data *between* agencies in the member states and outside the EU. A proposal was put forward by the Commission in October 2005. As at the end of June 2008, the measure is listed as ready for adoption by the Council.[71] Everyone but the Council is opposed to its content. The European Parliament, which only has powers of consultation (not of co-decision), insisted twice on being re-consulted as each time its views were routinely ignored. The European Data Protection Supervisor and the Article 29 Working Party on data protection (all the national Data Protection Commissioners) were strongly opposed to it, too. The reason for this was simple. When the Council got round to allocating the brief, it gave it not to the Working Party on Data Protection, but to the Multidisciplinary Group on Organised Crime (MDG) with representatives from national law enforcement agencies and Interior Ministries – a bit like 'putting the wolf in charge of the sheep'.[72]

Peter Hustinx, the European Data Protection Supervisor, said of the membership of the Multidisciplinary Group on Organised Crime:

'national delegations tend to come from law enforcement areas which, up to now, largely prefer to ignore data protection.'

While Lord Avebury (UK House of Lords Select Committee on the EU) said the MDG's:

'primary interest is to make life difficult for criminals, not to have regard to the interests of data subjects.'

As to the proposal itself, there are a number of issues which are not addressed at all. No distinction is made between 'hard data' (arrest, charge, conviction) and information better termed 'intelligence' of varying reliability, some of which is based on suspicions or speculation (described above). The European Data Protection Supervisor said this is a glaring omission: 'data based on facts' need to be distinguished from 'data based on opinion or personal assessment'.

How is access and data exchanged in relation to the 'handling codes' for intelligence used by Europol (and most other police forces)?[73] What if the source of the information is classified as either:

'from whom information received has in most instances proved to be unreliable' (1.C)
or *'the reliability of the source cannot be assessed' (1.D)*

and/or the 'reliability' is evaluated as:

'information which is not known personally to the source and cannot be corroborated.' (2.4)

Can this data be exchanged?

Second, no distinction is made between transferring data on criminals, suspects, victims and witnesses. Thus, data on non-suspects could be exchanged between agencies within the EU and outside.

Third, there are no limits on the holding of data transferred. The European Data Protection Authorities say that:

'Limited storage is a basic principle of data protection ... it should not be overridden simply because a Member State chooses to legislate otherwise.'

Fourth, for both hard data and intelligence there is no provision for 'spent sentences', after which data should be removed. As there are major differences between the laws in Member States, data could be transferred from a Member State where it was due to be deleted, but it could be retained by the requesting state for ever.

Substantive criticisms

The scope of the measure makes no distinction between serious crime and any crime, however minor. The European Data Protection Supervisor says that Article 3 (Principles of lawfulness, proportionality and purpose) is 'too broad'. He says:

'the purpose of police and judicial cooperation is not by its nature legitimate and certainly not specified'

and:

'it is not sufficient to start from the assumption that the police, under all circumstances and in all cases, operate within the legal limits of their legal obligations.'

The measure refers to 'automated processing' but is silent on 'automated access', which could be agreed between the 'competent authorities' at national level.[74] The measure does not cover 'national security', that is transfers to security and intelligence agencies – so is there going to be another measure setting out limits and protections on their use of data?

The measure would allow the exchange of data from EU 'information systems'. The measure is littered with references to 'national law', as if these would provide protection to individual rights. But, as has already been noted, no survey is available on the state of national laws. This is how 'bad' law is made. The European Data Protection Supervisor describes this well:

'to give a concrete example, this would mean that a law enforcement body at national or EU level when dealing with a criminal file – consisting of information from various, national, other Member States' and EU authorities – would have to apply different processing rules for different pieces of information depending on whether: personal data have been gathered domestically or not; each of the transmitting bodies has given its consent for the envisaged purpose; the storage is compliant with time limits laid down by applicable laws of each of the transmitting bodies; further processing restrictions requested by each of the transmitting bodies do not prohibit the processing; in case of a request from a third country, each transmitting body has given its consent according to its own evaluation of adequacy and/or international commitments. In addition, citizens' protection and rights will vary enormously, and be subject to different broad derogations, depending on the Member State where processing takes place'[75]

We can see how complex the process would be under the 'further processing' that is allowed. Member State 'A' collects data for purpose 'B', this is then accessed by Member State 'C' for purpose 'D', the data held by Member State 'C' is then transferred to Third State 'E' who passes it to agencies 'F', 'G' and 'H' who use it for purposes 'I', 'J' and

'K'. Such further processing is allowed, where the 'competent authorities' are 'authorised' by 'national law'.

When it comes to the transfer of personal data outside the EU the original proposal has simply been re-written to meet US demands. The US is on record on a number of occasions in the outcomes of EU-US meetings as saying that the imposition of an adequacy test:

'would jeopardise the informal excellent contacts developed over time by the US LEAs with their opposite numbers in the Member States.'

In the Multidisciplinary Group on Organised Crime discussions six EU states – Germany, Denmark, Spain, Ireland, Sweden and UK – plus Norway *'were opposed to the requirement for an adequacy finding.'*[76]

So, Article 27 states that the Framework decision shall not affect any existing bilateral or multilateral agreement with third states. No standard criteria or mechanism for adequacy of the protections given by third states is laid down. Findings of 'adequacy' are yet again left to 'national laws'. Most crucial of all are the rights of the data subject. Article 16 says that Member States shall ensure the data subject:

'is informed regarding the collection or processing of personal data by their competent authorities, in accordance with national law'.

This is *not* a commitment to inform the data subject every time information is gathered on them. It could simply be met by a statement of how data in general is processed by agencies. And there is a big get-out clause which says each Member State (the requesting and receiving) can:

'ask that the other Member State does not inform the data subject. In such a case the latter Member State shall not inform the data subject without the prior consent of the other Member State.'

As to the 'Right of access' (Article 17), this is dependent on the data subject making a 'request'. It is a 'right' that can only be exercised if a person is aware or suspects that their data is being processed. Response to a 'request' can be refused if it would 'prejudice' an investigation and 'for protecting national security'.

EU-US High Level Group report[77]
The EU and USA set up a 'High Level Group' to try and reach a permanent pact for all future agreements concerning data protection

and the exchange of data between the two blocs. All of the current EU-US agreements have raised contentious issues concerning the privacy right and data protection given by the USA for EU citizens. The 1974 US Privacy Act only applies to US citizens and, as Barry Steinhardt of the American Civil Liberties Union has observed, it contains:

'no oversight or legal protections for non-US persons. As a result, the communications of European citizens are completely vulnerable to abuse. We believe that this situation clearly violates European legal requirements for the fair and lawful processing of personal information.'

The scope would cover 'any criminal offence', however minor. There is no guarantee EU citizens will be informed that data and information on them has been transferred to the USA, or to which agencies it has been passed, or give them the right to correct it. Moreover, the agreement would apply to individual requests and automated mass transfers, and allow the USA to give the data to any third state 'if permitted under its domestic law'.

8

Case Study
EU-US cooperation

There are a number of milestones in EU-USA relations since 1945. NATO was set up in 1949, and embraced most of Western Europe. Alongside came the interventions of the CIA, especially in Italy, the Greek 'colonels' coup in 1974, and the creation of front organisations espousing 'Western values'.[78] The Vietnam War divided the USA and countries across the EU with massive demonstrations of opposition. There was great opposition, too, to the CIA and US counter-insurgency operations in Asia, Latin America and Africa,[79] just as there was opposition to the colonial wars fought by European states against liberation movements in Africa and Asia.

The end of the Cold War, in 1989, coincided with a recognition that globalisation was under way, a process which was quickly defined as necessitating 'free-market economics'. This was a definition which would always favour the powerful over the weak – with the 'West' (USA together with the EU and Japan) dictating terms to the third world.

By the 1990s, the USA was the hegemonic power in the world. In 1995, the USA met with EU leaders in Madrid and signed the New Transatlantic Agenda (NTA) and the Joint EU-US Action Plan, on 3 December.[80] In the same month G8 (founded in 1975) expanded its remit from economic issues to terrorism, organised crime and drugs at a meeting on 12 December in Ottawa, Canada.[81]

The Joint EU-US Action Plan speaks of 'global challenges' and 'building bridges across the Atlantic' by meeting the challenges of:

> *'international crime, terrorism and drug trafficking, mass migration, the degradation of the environment, nuclear safety and disease.'*

The Action Plan was followed up with meetings of the Senior Level Group and EU-US Task Force. Statewatch applied for the agendas of these meetings and, after more than four years and two successful complaints to the European Ombudsman, in the summer of 2001 got copies of very basic agendas from 1996 onwards – albeit with over 450 items deleted at the insistence of the USA.[82]

Everything changed after 11 September 2001. On 16 October 2001, President Bush sent a letter to the EU with 40 demands for action[83]. The invasion of Iraq by the USA and UK started on 20 March 2003. Dreadful bombings took place in Madrid in March 2004, and in London in July 2005.

There are currently six EU-US agreements covering justice and home affairs issues:
1. Europol (exchange of data)
2. Extradition
3. Mutual assistance
4. PNR (passenger name record)
5. SWIFT (all financial transactions, commercial and personal)
6. Container Security Initiative (CSI).

The ones on extradition and mutual assistance have yet to come into force.

There are 30 plus EU-US meetings on justice and home affairs during each six month EU Presidency with meetings of;
– JHA Troika Ministerial
– EU-USA JHA Senior Level
– EU-USA JHA High Level
– EU-USA Task Force.

All of the publicly available records of these meetings (known as 'Outcomes') have the views and demands of the US side deleted. However, below is a taste of what happens.

EU/US security 'channel' – a one-way street?

Since 11 September 2001, EU-US cooperation on justice and home affairs has reached unprecedented levels through what is termed the 'US/EU channel'. The Council Presidency of the EU ensures that the USA and its agencies are kept up to date with all the latest documents (e.g. Action Plans), and EU meetings and seminars are regularly attended by US officials.[84]

What the 'outcomes' of EU-US meetings show is the extraordinary influence that the US has on EU justice and home affairs policies and practice. The dominant theme is US demands for access to EU data, intelligence and databases and ensuring that US interests are not threatened (e.g. by EU data protection standards). There is also evidence of 'policy-laundering', where the US promotes initiatives through third bodies it would not advance at home.[85] For example, detailed G8 questionnaires drafted by the

US to which all EU governments have to respond (e.g. use of intelligence in criminal investigation and prosecution, EU doc no 12064/06).[86]

The 'US/EU channel' is largely a 'one-way street' for US demands. It is rarely used by the EU to meet its own needs and, when it does, it faces intransigency. One such issue is visa reciprocity – under the US Visa Waiver Programme (see below) only 15 EU countries do not have to apply for visas (the original 15 minus Greece but plus Slovenia). People from the other 12 EU countries still need to get a visa. At a meeting in Vienna on 3 May 2006, the EU Presidency said that visa reciprocity 'has become a crucial element in the relations between the EU and the USA.' On 'e-passports' the EU side said a great effort had gone into:

> *'complying by 26 August 2006, with the requirement set by the US (that is, to start issuing RFID digitised photo chips).'* (EU doc no: 9223/06)[87]

But, by a meeting in January 2007, despite a pledge by George Bush, the US came up front with a whole series of new demands before they would add 12 EU countries to the Visa Waiver Programme:

> *'airport security, air marshals, reporting on lost and stolen passports, passenger information exchange, electronic travel authorisation, etc.'* (EU doc no: 5655/07)[88]

But on the proposed EU travel 'exit-entry systems':

> *'the US side sees possibilities to exchange data in this field since entry data in one country corresponds to exit data for another country.'* (EU doc no: 5655/07)

The 'EU side' said, in relation to fingerprints collected for EU passports and for visas, that there was a:

> *'need for bilateral agreements before third countries could have access to fingerprint data (7618/06) but ... it further emphasised the importance of interoperability of systems, so as to ensure a full working access to all parties.'* (EU doc no: 9223/06)

And the US side:

> *'invited the EU to assess how access for verification into e-passport databases will be organised.'* (EU doc no: 9223/06)

And:

> *'the US side wished to explore the possibility of exchanging data with Eurodac, both for analysis and for searching for people.'* (EU doc no: 5655/07)

And:

'the US side asked that the architecture for SIS II be designed in a way that would not prevent future exchanges of information with third countries.' (EU doc no: 12064/06)

When the US side asked about access to telecommunications data, held by EU member states under the mandatory data retention directive, the EU side said there was no problem at all as this would be available under:

'existing MLA agreements (bilateral as well as EU/US agreement).' (EU doc no: 7618/06)[89]

The draft Framework Decision on data protection in police and judicial cooperation has been amended because:

'if adopted as it stands, it would jeopardise the informal excellent contacts developed over time by the US law enforcement agencies with their opposite numbers in the Member States.' (EU doc no: 12064/06)

But how is the recurring issue of the lack of data protection in the USA for EU citizens to be tackled? By the creation of a 'High Level Contact Group on data protection and data sharing' for which 'the US delegation handed over a Proposed Outline' of work.

How the United States gets its way

When the USA wanted the EU to sign up to its Container Security Initiative (CSI), to assess and check shipping containers bound for their country, the EU wanted time to consult. The USA simply by-passed the EU and reached bilateral agreements with a number of individual Member States, forcing the EU to reach a general agreement. The CSI currently operates from 21 European ports in 10 EU states.

The USA is now doing exactly the same over a long-standing issue with the EU – the Visa Waiver Programme (VWP). At present, citizens of only 15 of the 27 EU Member States are part of the VWP – the 15, minus Greece but plus Slovenia; the 12 'new' Member States are excluded. During 2006 and 2007, the EU said that all 27 states had to be treated the same.

It was obvious to EU negotiators by January 2008 that, having changed its laws, the USA intended to go behind its back and negotiate bilateral 'Memorandums of Understanding' (MOUs) with individual EU member states.[90] So alarmed was the EU – having got sight of the US MOUs – that a scheduled meeting, on 5 March 2008, of the Council's Mixed Committee (high-level officials dealing with Schengen issues) was taken over by COREPER (the committee comprised of the permanent representation of each government in Brussels).[91] A strongly-worded press release re-asserted that all EU member states should be treated equally, and that any agreement should be with the EU. It reminded the USA that there was already a EU-USA Passenger Name Record agreement and that:

'no additional requirements should be added.'

Notification of lost and stolen documents was already being made to Interpol, which 'should be sufficient', and:

'any extension of the reporting data to Interpol should be agreed commonly by the EU.'

Most significant of all was the simple statement:

'no commitments as to access for the US to EU/EC data bases or information systems.'

This suggested that the USA could get access to personal data held on the main EU databases like SIS and SIS II (Schengen Information System), VIS (Visa Information System with biometrics), Eurodac (fingerprints of asylum-seekers), CIS (Customs Information System) via a member state that had signed a Memorandum of Understanding with the USA.

Despite this intervention, seven member states have signed up so far: Czech Republic, Estonia, Hungary, Latvia, Malta and Slovakia; and there is an interim agreement with Bulgaria. As these MOUs became available it became obvious that their implications went far, far beyond the matter of issuing visas.[92]

On 9 April 2008, a proposal by the Council Presidency on a negotiating mandate for the Commission to reach an agreement with the USA was adopted by COREPER.[93] Significantly the negotiating mandate states, at the outset, that it:

'authorises the Commission to open negotiations for the conclusion of an agreement between the European Community and the United States of America regarding certain conditions for access to the US's Visa Waiver Program in accordance with Section 711 of the Implementing Recommendations of the 9/11 Commission Act of 2007.'

This begs the question of what does Section 711 of the 9/11 Act say? First, although under the heading 'Visa Waiver', the title of this Section is:

'Secure Travel and Counterterrorism Partnership Act 2007.'[94]

As we shall see, this is partly about visa travel and partly about 'counter-terrorism partnerships'. So it comes as no surprise that the first objective is enhancing 'security requirements', but the second is:

'extending visa-free travel privileges to nationals of foreign countries that are partners in the war on terrorism – that are actively cooperating with the United States to prevent terrorist travel, including sharing counter-terrorism and law enforcement information.'

Moreover, the US Secretary for Homeland Security has to be satisfied that a:

'country's participation in the program would not compromise the law enforcement, security interests or the enforcement of the immigration laws of the United States.'

The scope of the Memorandums of Understanding signed by EU member states and any agreement negotiated by the Commission goes much, much further than the issuing of visas. This intent was made absolutely clear in a statement by Richard Barth, Assistant Secretary for Policy Development, Department of Homeland Security, to the US House of Representatives' Committee on Foreign Affairs, on 14 May 2008.[95] He told the Committee that the programme:

'creates tremendous incentives for VWP aspirants to enhance their security standards and deepen their cooperation with the United States on security-related issues.'

The Memorandums of Understanding, or agreements, would cover 'passenger information, serious crimes, known or suspected terrorists, asylum and migration matters', and the majority of countries would conclude agreements:

'to share their known or suspected terrorist watch-lists.'

Finally, he said that DHS-led interagency teams had visited the Czech Republic, Estonia, Greece, Hungary and Slovakia – and planned to visit Latvia and Lithuania – to:

'comprehensively review their counter-terrorism capabilities; immigration, citizenship and naturalisation laws; passport production and issuance controls; efforts to combat crime; law enforcement cooperation with the USA; border control mechanisms.'

These issues are only marginally, at best, connected to the issuing of visas; rather, they are a concerted attempt to impose US standards and, most crucially, to gain access to national and EU databases and intelligence.[96]

All the EU-USA agreements are supposedly based on 'reciprocity' (equal rights for both sides of the agreement). Imagine the EU sending officials to the USA to 'comprehensively' review the work of the FBI, CIA, NSA and the DHS before it agreed to any EU member state or the EU centrally transferring any information/intelligence. For example, by looking at the adequacy of data protection offered, the agencies to which the data is passed, what further processing happens, and to which third countries is the data passed.[97] The agreements in place cover not only the passing of data/intelligence from the EU to the USA, but also the passing of data from the USA to EU databases – a personal file originating in the EU could be passed to US agencies who further process it (add data or intelligence) and send it back to the EU.

Observations

EU governments and officials claim that 'Europe and the United States share common values' and there is no doubt that, for the most part, governments and officials believe this. There is little doubt, too, that this is the view of the multinationals, the law enforcement, security and intelligence agencies, and the military. On the other hand, many in the EU believe it should be friendly to the USA but maintain a distinctive 'European' position in world affairs, while others believe working closely with the USA, not least given its repugnant actions in the 'war on terrorism', is disastrous both for Europe and the future of the world. Equally, there are many people in Europe and the USA who do believe we have 'common values', but not the values of our governments.

9

Conclusions

The new programme, scheduled to be called the 'Stockholm' programme, will be adopted by the European Council – a meeting of all the Prime Ministers from the 27 member states – and will 'set in stone' the priorities for home affairs for the following five years.

The 'convergence principle' and 'state-building'[98]

The introduction of the 'convergence principle' is another step in the building of the EU state. This is described in the background papers for the Future Group as '*the pooling of sovereignty*'. It builds on the 'principle of availability' (Hague programme) of all data, information and intelligence held by all agencies across the EU to all other agencies and outside, and the 'interoperability' of EU information systems must be compatible so that all agencies can access each other's data

'Convergence' means shifting from harmonising laws at national level to standardising training, equipment and information technology across all the law enforcement agencies in the EU. This ensures 'interoperability' and efficiency, and is much cheaper if EU-wide standards are set and then licences are negotiated with the multinationals. Agencies will still work at the national level, but their environment will be determined (harmonised) by EU standards, and more and more roles will be undertaken at the EU level. 'Convergence' also requires further legal harmonisation so that 'obstacles' (e.g. judicial authorisation) to gathering, accessing and transferring data and intelligence are removed.

In the Lisbon Treaty 'state-building' is evident in both the creation of bodies and agencies to act on an EU-wide basis, and the creation of administrative and operational cooperation centrally organised by the EU. 'Cooperation' will cover all 'criminal offences' and embrace all agencies. This will include the establishment of measures for the 'collection, storage, processing, analysis and exchange of relevant information' and for 'investigative techniques' (which means telephone-tapping, bugging, informants, agent provocateurs, etc).[99]

Overseeing operational activities will be the new Standing Committee on Internal Security (COSI), which is planned to oversee and direct all operational matters – with national and European parliaments only to be 'informed' about its activities.[100]

This analysis only deals with certain aspects of EU state-building, those concerning justice and home affairs and internal security. Another aspect is the proposed European External Action Service, envisaged under the Lisbon Treaty, which would turn the current European Commission 180 plus missions around the world into EU embassies with powers of intelligence-gathering.

Yet another example is the EU Security Research Agenda. This is described, in what should be viewed as a complementary study to this one, in *Arming Big Brother* as:

> '*the development of the security-industrial complex in Europe and in particular the development of the EU Security Research Programme (ESRP). Spawned by the military-industrial complex, the security-industrial complex has developed as the traditional boundaries between external security (military) and internal security (security services) and law enforcement (policing) have eroded.*'[101]

The 'digital tsunami and the EU surveillance state'

The coded language in the main Future Group report hides the broader intent that is revealed in other documents, especially the one from the Portuguese Council Presidency. The assumption behind the 'digital tsunami' is:

> '*every object the individual uses, every transaction they make and almost everywhere they go will create a detailed digital record. This will generate a wealth of information for public security organisations, and create huge opportunities for more effective and productive public security efforts.*'

The implications of this statement are breathtaking.

Across the EU – following the 2004 EU directive – governments have, or are, adopting national laws for the mandatory retention of everyone's communications data, all forms of communication (phone calls, faxes, mobile calls including locations). This will be extended to keeping a record of all internet usage from 2009 – even though few are aware this is happening.[102] This allows law enforcement and security agencies to get access to all traffic data – in the UK access is already automated. Access to the content should, under national law, be authorised by judicial authorities – though state agencies have had the technological capability to access content for years.

When traffic data including internet usage is combined with other data held by the state, or gathered from non-state sources (tax, employment, bank details, credit card usage, biometrics, criminal record, health record, use of e-government services, travel history, etc) plus 'open source' information, a frighteningly detailed picture of each individual's everyday life and habits can be accessed at the click of a button.[103]

The harnessing of the 'digital tsunami' by public security organisations, as set out in the Portuguese Council Presidency's paper, means that behaviour will be predicted and assessed by 'machines' on the basis of which directions are given to state officials on the spot.

To this must be added the fact that state agencies can access any home or work computer and look at its contents – and, if they can look at its content, they could add or alter it too. It was a proposal by the German government in June 2008 that confirmed the ability of the agencies to do this, by seeking the power to authorise online computer searches in private homes through:

'remote searches of computer hard drives.'[104]

Taking all these extensive powers of surveillance together, it is not too hard to see, for example, why lawyers, journalists and civil society groups might be concerned. The monitoring of a lawyer's communications and correspondence could reveal the defence's case and counter-evidence gathered – especially in cases which are politically sensitive. A journalist's contacts and communications could be watched in order to pre-empt a story or to prepare a plausible denial in advance. While a group organising a protest could find its preparatory work undermined and disrupted, and its organisers targeted for detention or arrest – with their demonstrations surveilled by spying 'drones'.[105]

'Ordinary' people who 'have nothing to hide' are under the illusion that this sweeping surveillance system has nothing to do with them – which is why they will never realise they did not get a job interview because the employer had accessed to a criminal record based on a 'spent' conviction, or why their application for an insurance policy failed because the company had access to their health record. The European Data Protection Supervisor put it politely when he said of the police and, by implication, all state agencies:

'it is not sufficient to start from the assumption that the police under all circumstances, and in all cases, operate within the legal limits of their legal obligations.'

There is an assumption, on this and wider issues in the EU, that 'if it is technologically possible, why should it not be introduced?' This brings to mind the discussion in the EU over the age at which children should be subjected to fingerprinting for passports, visas or ID cards. The discussions in the working parties of the Council of the European Union (the governments) have been based not on moral questions, but rather at what age is it technologically possible to collect accurate fingerprints. Most want this to be from six years old and upwards, but some even want to collect them at birth.[106]

At the heart of this issue is the 'ownership' of personal data. Is it our personal data, which we 'own' and which we may consent to be used for a specific, stated purpose? Or is it 'owned' by the collector and holder of the data (internet service provider, airline, bank or credit card companies, or state agencies)? For example, the European Parliament is currently discussing a proposal from the Commission on users' rights relating to electronic communications networks. The European Data Protection Supervisor has raised the question of whether Internet Protocol addresses ('IP') are personal data, as the Data Protection Directive and the Privacy Directive apply whenever personal data are processed, but:

> *'if IP addresses are not deemed personal data they can be collected and further processed without the need to fulfil any legal obligation arising from the two above mentioned Directives. For example, such an outcome would enable a search engine to store, for an indefinite period, IP addresses assigned to accounts from which, for example, materials related to specific health conditions (e.g.: AIDS) have been searched.'[107]*

It will be remembered that, under the EU Directive on mandatory data retention, all internet service providers are obliged, from 2009, to store records of all internet usage by everyone in Europe. What if searches for 'specific health conditions' are captured and stored by ISPs, then accessed by state agencies and further processed by them – who 'owns' this data, the individual or the state?

The security-industrial nexus

In the immediate aftermath of 11 September 2001, the EU and national governments adopted measures said to be 'exceptional' but necessary because of the 'war on terrorism', and that they were not permanent but time limited. Seven years on the 'exceptional' has become the norm.

What is much clearer now is that 11 September 2001 was used to accelerate a process already under way. Globalisation and its 'technological revolution' – nurtured by Western states and developed by multinationals – was ready to break out of the constraints imposed by liberal democratic values. Notions of privacy and data protection, espoused as basic values, stood in the way of progress. The welfare state, where a benevolent state protected and cared for the people, has been replaced by the market state, requiring the social control of market forces unhindered by rights and regulations. In place of theoretically serving the people, the state now serves the interests of international capital.

Moreover, the 'war on terrorism' presented a massive opportunity, not only to use its monopoly of information technology, but also to apply it to new, highly lucrative areas: the surveillance of travel and communications, new systems for data-sharing, data-mining, interpreting behaviour, the collection of biometrics and readers to check them. The construction of EU-US standards to record, check and hold people's travel records, is intended to set standards which will be laundered to set global standards – and new markets for the West's multinationals to pursue and profit from.

EU-USA

Internationally, the prospects are little better. It is often forgotten that 21 of the 27 Member States of the EU are also in NATO, which is why the majority are supplying 'peace-making' or 'peace-keeping' troops in Afghanistan. Through NATO and other fora, the influence of the USA on the EU has grown enormously since 2001. The most significant, largely unseen, influence has been through the numerous high-level meetings between the EU and the USA on justice and home affairs issues. All the evidence shows that this is an unequal relationship with nearly all the demands coming from the US side.

Top EU officials are fond of saying the EU and the USA share 'common values', but do we? What they mean is that the political élites (governments and officials) share the same values.

Now the Future Group is proposing that the EU finally 'make up its mind' (i.e. it has already been discussed) by 2014, on the creation of a:

> *'Euro-Atlantic area of cooperation with the USA in the field of Freedom, Security and Justice.'*

This goes way beyond the existing mechanisms for cooperation. Since

2001, six agreements have been reached with the USA – all of them controversial. High-level officials have been meeting regularly, though these meetings concern specific issues, *not* every aspect of justice and home affairs. The Future Group's 'area of cooperation' would cover *all* aspects of justice and home affairs: policing and terrorism, immigration, asylum and border controls, laws and rights of suspects, databases and data-sharing, privacy and data protection. The USA would be sitting at the table with a very powerful voice, with its demands and influence hidden from public view.[108]

The politics of EU values

One of the myths that the EU seeks to perpetuate is the idea that it is based on 'common values'. Amongst these are 'freedom', 'justice', 'fundamental rights' and in this context 'privacy' (and data protection). In practice these values have changing meanings according to the general political climate. For example, the 'values' of the EU are not the same as they were in 2000, when Austria's membership of the EU was suspended under the Treaty because of the inclusion in its government of a fascist and racist party. If the EU still had the same 'values' then the membership of the Italian government could have been suspended this summer over its policies of targeting, detaining and deporting Roma with overt racist statements.

Are the 'shared/common values' of the EU the same now as they were in 1999? In 1999, there were 15 EU member states with 12 governments on the broad left (social democrats) and 3 on the right – now with 27 member states there are 21 on the right or far-right and only 6 on the so-called 'left'(social democrats) including the UK! What this means is that the 'Council of the European Union' (the governments) is in the hands of the right and far-right, and that the mandates given by Interior and Justice Ministries at national level to officials and officers going to Council working parties reflect their politics. While in the European Parliament the PPE (Conservative Group), and its allies, are the largest coalition and, after the 2009 European elections, may well be in outright control for five years.

The European Summit (dominated by the centre and far-right) will lay down the new justice and home affairs programme, and the Council of the European Union, through the Justice and Home Affairs Council (dominated by the centre and far-right), will, as it always does, have the final say on the content of each and every measure.

In the European Parliament the centre-right and its far-right allies can put together the largest parliamentary block, which can only be defeated if all the other groups (PSE, Socialist, ALDE, Liberal, Green and GUE, united left) vote together – which happens occasionally. With the European Parliament elections in June 2009, there is a possibility that the centre-right and far-right will have a permanent majority.[109]

EU 'values' are not 'shared' or 'common', but are those of the ruling élite who assume they can define and propagate as a 'consensus' where there is none.

Final comment

'There is now only a slim chance that the political élites in the Council of the European Union, the European Commission, national governments, the law enforcement agencies and the multinationals will change course – they have already invested too much to allow a meaningful public debate to take place.

This is because they actually believe that technology, not values and morality, should drive change. They believe they have balanced freedom and security, when all with eyes and ears to see and hear know that liberties and freedoms have been made subservient to the demands of security.

The national and European states require unfettered powers to access and gather masses of personal data on the everyday life of everyone, so that we can all be safe and secure from perceived 'threats'. But how are we to be safe from the state itself, from its uses and abuses of the data they hold on us?

The outrageous proposal that the EU should tie itself in with the USA across the whole justice and home affairs field will place our privacy and civil liberties in great danger.

If we do not have an open and meaningful debate now we never will, because by then it will be too late.'

Thanks to the Network for Social Change for their financial support in preparing this publication: http://thenetworkforsocialchange.org.uk/

Thanks to Ben Hayes, Steve Peers, Trevor Hemming, Heiner Busch and Ann Singleton for their comments and help.

Tony Bunyan is a writer and journalist and has been Director of *Statewatch* since 1991. He is the author of *The Political Police in Britain* (1977), *Secrecy and Openness in the EU* (1999) and has edited numerous *Statewatch* publications including *The War on Freedom and Democracy – Essays on Civil Liberties in Europe* (2006). He has taken eight successful complaints against the Council of the European Union to the

European Ombudsman on access to documents on behalf of *Statewatch*, as well as two successful complaints against the European Commission. In 2001 and 2004, he was selected by the *European Voice* newspaper as one of the 50 most influential people in Europe.

References

1 With due acknowledgement to H G Wells. 'The Shape of Things to Come' was written by Wells in 1933, and he wrote the screenplay for the film 'Things to Come' in 1936. Among other things he predicted a 'technological revolution' which would be used by the state in a highly authoritarian way. However, he was trying to envisage what the world would look like in 2106 – not 2008.

Thanks to the Network for Social Change for their support: http://thenetworkforsocialchange.org.uk/

2 Future Group report: *Freedom, Security and Privacy – the area of European Home Affairs*: http://www.statewatch.org/news/2008/jul/eu-futures-jha-report.pdf

3 Timetable: http://www.statewatch.org/news/2008/jul/eu-futures-plan-2007-2009.pdf

4 'Terms of reference': http://www.statewatch.org/news/2008/jul/eu-futures-terms-of-ref.pdf Meetings were prepared by prior meetings of 'Sherpas' designated by each participant.

5 The report on 'justice' was produced by the 'High Level Advisory Group on the Future of European Justice Policy' entitled: 'Proposed Solutions for the Future EU Justice Programme': http://www.statewatch.org/news/2008/jul/eu-futures-justice-report.pdf. The Justice Future Group was comprised of same nine Council Presidencies as the 'European Home Affairs' group, with Ireland as the 'common law' observer.

6 The Council of the European Union is comprised of representatives of the 27 national governments (Ministers and officials).

7 The Observer from the EP Civil Liberties Committee (LIBE) was Jean-Marie Cavada until January 2008, Gerard Deprez from January 2008.

8 There is certainly a case for dividing up the current DG AFSJ in the Commission. Data protection was transferred from DG Internal Market and 'fundamental rights' was later put in this DG – both seemingly to justify the 'Freedom' in AFSJ. Neither unit sits happily in this DG when down the corridor people's privacy is being buried in measure after measure to serve the law enforcement agencies not the rights of the people. There should be a DG 'Home Affairs', DG 'Justice' and a new DG 'Rights' covering data protection, fundamental rights and EU ombudsmen.

9 Tampere programme full-text:
http://www.statewatch.org/news/2003/sep/tamp.htm

10 The story of Tampere: an undemocratic process excluding civil society:
http://www.statewatch.org/news/2003/sep/tampere.pdf

11 From Maastricht to The Hague: the politics of judicial and police cooperation by Charles Elsen. ERA Forum (2007) 8: 13-26.

12 The latest annual report from the UK Chief Surveillance Commissioner shows that there were 519,000 accesses largely by law enforcement agencies in the UK for whom access is automated so there is no process of regulation. Over 400 local authorities also have access.

13 *Lex Vigilatoria – Towards a control system without a state?* by Thomas Mathiesen: http://www.ecln.org/essays/essay-7.pdf

14 SIS II *fait accompli*? Construction of EU's Big Brother database underway:
http://www.statewatch.org/analyses/no-45-sisII-analysis-may05.pdf

15 EU: Cementing the European state – new emphasis on internal security and operational cooperation at EU level:
http://www.statewatch.org/news/2008/feb/07lisbon-european-state.htm

16 Statewatch: 'Scoreboard' on post-Madrid counter-terrorism plans:
http://www.statewatch.org/news/eu-plan.pdf

17 Only Austria, Finland, Ireland, Sweden, Cyprus and Malta are not in NATO.

18 Arming Big Brother: http://www.statewatch.org/analyses/bigbrother.pdf

19 Summary of 'Warm-up' Session, Eltville (Germany), 20 and 21 May 2007 Report: http://www.statewatch.org/news/2008/jul/eu-futures-may-report-2007.pdf

20 Introductory Document: Modernising European border and visa management – 21 May 2007: http://www.statewatch.org/news/2008/jul/eu-futures-may-borders-2007.pdf; Comprehensive European Migration Policy: http://www.statewatch.org/news/2008/jul/eu-futures-oct-migration-2007.pdf; The future EU Asylum policy: Sweden and Czech Republic: http://www.statewatch.org/news/2008/jul/eu-futures-apr-asylum-2008.pdf

21 Killing me softly? 'Improving access to durable solutions': doublespeak and the dismantling of refugee protection in the EU: http://www.statewatch.org/analyses/no-29-eu-ref-ext-process.pdf

22 See: http://www.statewatch.org/news/2008/jul/eu-futures-apr-asylum-2008.pdf

23 UK: Mobility, Security and Privacy:
http://www.statewatch.org/news/2008/jul/eu-futures-dec-uk-sec-mobility-2007.pdf

24 Since 1925 there has been a Common Travel Area between the Republic of Ireland and the UK. The UK Home Office is proposing to introduce border controls and biometric checks. Consultation: http://www.statewatch.org/news/2008/jul/uk-ireland-border-checks-consult.pdf

25 Under the last UK Conservative government there was even a period when

all people had to do to enter was to 'wave' their passports at border officials.
26 Within the Schengen area most people travel using their national identity cards so discussion has started on standardising fingerprinting rules.
27 Final Report by EU-US High Level Contact Group on information sharing and privacy and personal data protection: http://www.statewatch.org/news/2008/jun/eu-usa-data-sharing-privacy-hlg-9831-08.pdf
28 There are already the following agreements between the EU and USA which affect the data protection rights of EU citizens: 1) Exchange of data/intelligence with Europol; 2) Extradition; 3) Mutual assistance – concrete cases involving the exchange of data and active investigation; 4) EU-PNR and 5) SWIFT.
29 American Civil Liberties Union (ACLU) Letter to the President of the EU Article 29 Data Protection Working Party: http://www.statewatch.org/news/2008/apr/aclu-eu-dp-letter.pdf
30 France: Police Cooperation: http://www.statewatch.org/news/2008/jul/eu-futures-apr-police-cooperation-2008.pdf
31 Germany: 5/2007/DE: http://www.statewatch.org/news/2008/jul/eu-futures-june-internal-sec-2007.pdf; and 4/2007/DE: Responses to blurriness between external and internal security: http://www.statewatch.org/news/2008/jul/eu-futures-june-internal-external-sec-2007.pdf
32 Global 'policing' role for EU: http://www.statewatch.org/news/2008/aug/nonmil.pdf
33 For a list see: http://www.statewatch.org/news/2008/jul/eu-futures-june-internal-sec-2007.pdf
34 EGF Treaty: http://www.statewatch.org/news/2007/oct/eu-gendarmerie-treaty-sept-2007.pdf
European Gendarmerie Force (EGF) launched in Italy on 19 January 2006: http://www.statewatch.org/news/2006/jan/03eu-gendarmarie.htm
35 Implementation of the external dimension of the area of freedom, security and justice: http://www.statewatch.org/news/2008/jul/eu-futures-june-external-2007.pdf
36 Report of the High Level Advisory Group on the future of EU Home Affairs Policies: http://www.statewatch.org/news/2008/jan/eu-future-group-report.pdf
37 Executive Summary & Final Report: http://www.statewatch.org/news/2008/jul/eu-futures-jha-report.pdf and EU doc no: 11960/08: http://www.statewatch.org/news/2008/aug/eu-futures-police-and-immigration-11960-08.pdf
38 Statewatch had, by 1997, taken six complaints against the Council (the governments) to the European Ombudsman and won all of them.
39 See 'Death of the Directive' by Paul Clarke in *Focus*, the journal of the European Information Association, March 2008.

40 Commission: Report on the implementation of the Hague Programme for 2007, COM (2008) 373 final, 2.7.08: http://www.statewatch.org/news/2008/jul/eu-com-hague-programme-implementation.pdf

41 See, Statewatch: 'Scoreboard' on post-Madrid counter-terrorism plans: http://www.statewatch.org/news/eu-plan.pdf

42 EU doc no: 11960/08: http://www.statewatch.org/news/2008/aug/eu-futures-police-and-immigration-11960-08.pdf

43 The principle of availability: http://www.statewatch.org/analyses/no-59-p-of-a-art.pdf

44 Secret trilogues and the democratic deficit: http://www.statewatch.org/analyses/no-64-secret-trilogues.pdf

45 Detection technologies and democracy: 'The quality of democratic life is too important to be decided by multinationals and the law enforcement and security agencies': http://www.statewatch.org/analyses/no-56-democracy-and-technology.pdf

46 The 1947 UKUSA agreement also includes Canada, New Zealand and Australia. It services a global intelligence network including the National Security Agency (USA) and Government Communications HQ (UK). The same network also runs ECHELON: a global communications interception (COMINT) system set up by the USA, UK, Canada, Australia and New Zealand to monitor and record all forms of electronic communications worldwide: http://www.statewatch.org/news/2005/may/steve-wright-stoa-rep.pdf

47 It will be recalled that there was an enormous outcry when it was learned that the USA was routinely accessing personal data on financial transfers through the SWIFT banking system.

48 European Gendarmerie Force (EUROGENDFOR): Treaty text: http://www.statewatch.org/news/2007/oct/eu-gendarmerie-treaty-sept-2007.pdf

49 For examples of third world outrage at the Returns Directive see: Morales article in the Guardian: http://www.guardian.co.uk/commentisfree/2008/jun/16/eu.immigration/print; Central American states reject EU Returns Directive: http://www.statewatch.org/news/2008/jul/PRONUNCIAMIENTO.pdf

50 EU/Africa: Carnage continues as EU border moves south, Yasha Maccanico: http://www.statewatch.org/analyses/no-55-immigration-analysis.pdf

51 EU divided over list of 'safe countries of origin' – *Statewatch* calls for the list to be scrapped: http://www.statewatch.org/analyses/no-38-safe-countries.pdf

52 Examining the creation of a European Border Surveillance System (EUROSUR) (COM 68 2008): http://www.statewatch.org/news/2008/feb/eu-com-68-08-eurosur.pdf

53 See: EU: 'safe and dignified', voluntary or 'forced' repatriation to 'safe' third countries & IOM: http://www.statewatch.org/news/2002/nov/14safe.htm

54 'Libya called on the European Union to revise new rules against illegal immigration on Monday, saying it would urge African Union members to take action if the EU stuck by measures that treated African migrants as criminals': http://africa.reuters.com/top/news/usnBAN525269.html
55 See Case study below.
56 A classic instance is EU-USA discussions over the Visa Waiver Programme which excludes 12 EU states. The EU thought it had an agreement but the US changed its laws and announced that it is going to negotiate 'Memorandum of Understanding' (MOUs) with individual Member States despite the EU's request that this should be agreed on behalf of all EU states. See: Outcomes of EU-US informal JHA senior level meeting (09-10 January 2008, Ljubljana): http://www.statewatch.org/news/2008/aug/eu-usa-jan-08-meet-5172.pdf
57 Concept paper on the European strategy to transform public security organizations in a connected world: http://www.statewatch.org/news/2008/jul/eu-futures-dec-sec-privacy-2007.pdf
58 During the Portuguese Council Presidency a Conference was held on 'RFID – The next step to The Internet of Things' (15-16 November 2007), EU doc no: 14681/07: http://www.statewatch.org/news/2007/nov/eu-rfid-of-things.pdf German Council Presidency in the first half of 2007: Working document for the expert conference 'RFID: Towards the Internet of Things', June 2007: http://www.statewatch.org/news/2008/jul/eu-rfid-of-things-germany.pdf
59 Under its Communications Data Bill the UK government is proposing to create one massive database of all communications including phones, mobiles and Internet usage in perpetuity.
60 See: Observatory on Data Protection: http://www.statewatch.org/eu-dp.htm
61 COSI – Standing Committee on Internal Security rescued from the debris of the EU Constitution: http://www.statewatch.org/news/2005/sep/08eu-cosi.htm
62 The second sentence of this quote was deleted after the Informal JHA meeting in Cannes.
63 'The essentials of a European information network in 2014': http://www.statewatch.org/news/2008/jul/eu-futures-oct-jha-2007.pdf
64 Framework Decision on simplifying the exchange of information between LEAs. OJ L 386/89, 29.12.06.
65 Prüm Treaty – full-text: http://www.statewatch.org/news/2005/aug/Pr%FCm-Convention.pdf; and Council Decision on cross-border cooperation, particularly in combating terrorism and cross-border crime: http://www.statewatch.org/news/2008/aug/eu-prum-decision-cross-border-coop-11896-07.pdf
66 Report by the Friends of the Presidency on the technical modalities to implement the principle of availability: http://www.statewatch.org/news/2008/aug/eu-fop-p-of-a-13558-rev1-05.pdf
67 Replies to questionnaire on Framework Decision on simplifying the exchange

of information and intelligence between law enforcement authorities of the member States of the European Union, in particular as regards serious offences including terrorist acts: http://www.statewatch.org/news/2008/aug/eu-49-sets-of-polce-data-5815-rev3.05.pdf Not only is the document not publicly available, two later versions, REV 2 and REV 3 are not even listed on the Council register.

68 EU police handling codes for intelligence: http://www.statewatch.org/news/2008/aug/04eu-police-handling-codes.htm

69 EU doc no: 8857/03: http://www.statewatch.org/news/2008/aug/eu-databases-8857-03.pdf

70 There are 22 Member states which are fully in Schengen – the exceptions are UK, Ireland, Romania, Bulgaria and Cyprus. These five never 'signed an agreement' exactly – their position results from the Schengen Protocol and the 2003 and 2005 accession treaties. Two non-Member States (Norway and Iceland) participate fully; an agreement with Switzerland is in force but not yet applied; and an agreement with Liechtenstein has been signed but not yet ratified.

71 EU data protection in police and judicial cooperation matters: Rights of suspects and defendants under attack by law enforcement demands: http://www.statewatch.org/news/2006/oct/eu-dp.pdf

72 The MDG has also been given the EU-PNR plan and after a few months discussion has again thrown the Commission proposal out of the window and are about to re-write it: http://www.statewatch.org/news/2008/jul/eu-pnr-austria-note-11724-08.pdf

73 EU police handling codes for intelligence: http://www.statewatch.org/news/2008/aug/04eu-police-handling-codes.htm

74 In the UK for 12 months in 2007-2008 there were over 500,000 automated accesses, largely by LEAs, to communication data. Annual report of the Chief Surveillance Commissioner. This compares to 360,000 in the previous 12 month period.

75 OJ C 139, 23.6.2007. The EDPS concludes that '*the legislative quality of the text is unsatisfactory.. This proposal would need substantial improvements before it could be the basis for the discussion of an adequate general framework*'.

76 EU doc: http://www.statewatch.org/news/2008/aug/eu-mdg-fd-dp-12924-06.pdf

77 Final Report by EU-US High Level Contact Group on information sharing and privacy and personal data protection: http://www.statewatch.org/news/2008/jun/eu-usa-data-sharing-privacy-hlg-9831-08.pdf

78 A number of CIA interventions were recorded in Statewatch's predecessor, *State Research* in the 1970s and early 1980s. For example, 'How NATO funds a press service', vol 3 no 3, 1979; 'The Institute for the Study of Conflict', vol 1 no 1, 1997; 'The origins and structure of NATO', vol 3 no 2, 1979.

79 For a renowned accounting of their activity see *CIA Diary* by the late Philip Agee.

80 EU-US Summit, Madrid, 3 December 1995: 'the New Transatlantic Agenda and the Joint EU-US Action Plan':
http://www.statewatch.org/news/2008/aug/eu-usa-nta-1995.pdf

81 At the meeting the UK's position was expressed as being concerned: *'not just about those engaged in terrorist activities but about other political activists who promoted unconstitutional change or destroyed the good relations enjoyed by the UK with other governments'.*

82 *'Secrecy and Openness in the European Union'* by Tony Bunyan (2003), an online book detailing the history of access to documents in the EU and the struggles by civil society to get proper freedom of information:
http://www.statewatch.org/secret/freeinfo/index.html

83 Bush letter to EU, 16 October 2001:
http://www.statewatch.org/news/2001/nov/06Ausalet.htm

84 For US influence on the EU through G8 see: The exceptional and draconian become the norm: http://www.statewatch.org/analyses/no-42-exceptional-and-draconian.pdf

85 Policy Laundering project: http://www.policylaundering.org/

86 EU doc: http://www.statewatch.org/news/2008/aug/eu-usa-12064-06.pdf

87 EU doc: http://www.statewatch.org/news/2008/aug/eu-usa-9223-06.pdf

88 EU doc: http://www.statewatch.org/news/2008/aug/eu-usa-5655-07.pdf

89 EU doc: http://www.statewatch.org/news/2008/aug/eu-usa-7618-06.pdf

90 See: Outcomes of EU-US informal JHA senior level meeting (09-10 January 2008, Ljubljana): http://www.statewatch.org/news/2008/aug/eu-usa-jan-08-meet-5172.pdf

91 Outcomes:http://www.statewatch.org/news/2008/mar/eu-us-visa-waiver-decision.pdf with an accompanying Council Press release:
http://www.statewatch.org/news/2008/mar/eu-us-visa-waiver.pdf

92 US-Czech MOU signed in February 2008:
http://www.statewatch.org/news/2008/mar/us-czech-mou-visas-etc.pdf

93 Text of negotiating mandate: http://www.statewatch.org/news/2008/jul/eu-us-visas-mandate-com.pdf

94 Section 711: http://www.statewatch.org/news/2008/jul/eu-usa-visas-section-711-text.pdf

95 See: http://www.statewatch.org/news/2008/jul/eu-usa-visas-barth-statement-may-2008.pdf

96 It is interesting to note that the UK government has threatened 11 countries that unless they change their policies on deportations or removals of their nationals and cooperate on crime and terrorism then their citizens visiting the UK will have to get visas. These are: Bolivia; Botswana; Brazil; Lesotho; Malaysia; Mauritius; Namibia; South Africa; Swaziland; Trinidad and Tobago; and Venezuela. These countries have a combined population of over 300 million. Brazil, Malaysia and Venezuela are on the European Commission's 'white list' of countries not requiring visas. Home Office press

release: http://www.statewatch.org/news/2008/jul/uk-visas-tests.pdf

97 The best estimate the EU's Article 29 Working Party on data protection could get was around 1,500 agencies in the USA.

98 That a European state is under construction is not a question – it is matter of whether you want to see it or not. Most of academia cannot see it, those at the sharp end – refugees, migrants and protestors – know it exists. In March 1991 – the same month Statewatch was launched – I wrote an article for *Race & Class*, 'Towards an authoritarian European state', nothing has happened since to change my view.

99 Cementing the European state – new emphasis on internal security and operational cooperation at EU level: http://www.statewatch.org/news/2008/feb/07lisbon-european-state.htm

100 The practice of 'informing' parliaments is no substitute for proper accountability. In the EU this usually means a bland annual report and an uninformed debate.

101 *Arming Big Brother* by Ben Hayes (TNI/Statewatch): http://www.statewatch.org/analyses/bigbrother.pdf

102 Statewatch Observatory: The surveillance of telecommunications in the EU: http://www.statewatch.org/eu-data-retention.htm

103 Open source spying: http://cryptome.org/cia-openspy.htm

104 German government press release: http://www.statewatch.org/news/2008/jun/germany-surveillance-powers-proposal-prel.pdf

105 See: Policing protests in Switzerland, Italy and Germany: http://www.statewatch.org/news/2008/apr/02policing-protests.htm and: Proposal to create EU-wide 'troublemakers' database: http://www.statewatch.org/news/2008/apr/04eu-troublemakers.htm

106 Fingerprinting of children: http://www.statewatch.org/news/2006/aug/02eu-fingerprinting-children.htm

107 Comments by the EDPS: http://www.statewatch.org/news/2008/sep/ep-eprivacy-edps-opinion.pdf

108 Official EU documents recording EU-US meetings are censored so that all the views expressed by the US are deleted: See: 'Partially accessible' document: http://www.statewatch.org/news/2008/sep/eu-usa-partial-access-9223-06.pdf and full-text doc: http://www.statewatch.org/news/2008/aug/eu-usa-9223-06.pdf

109 Surge in support for far right ahead of poll reflects centre-left crisis across EU: Guardian, link: http://www.guardian.co.uk/world/2008/sep/25/eu/print

Documentation

All the documents (and any future documents) are available on:
Statewatch: Observatory on 'The Shape of Things to Come' – the EU
Future Group: http://www.statewatch.org/future-group.htm

Contact information
Statewatch office: 00 44 0208 802 1882
e-mail: office@statewatch.org
Postal address: Statewatch, PO Box 1516, London N16 0EW, UK

Abbreviations

ACLU – American Civil Liberties Union
ACP – African, Caribbean and Pacific
AFSJ –Area of Freedom, Security and Justice
ALDE – Alliance of Liberal Democrats for Europe
CCTV – Closed Circuit Television
CECIS–Common European and Coordination Information System
CEPOL – European Police College
CIA – Central Intelligence Agency
CIS – Customs Information System
COMINT – Communications Intelligence
COREPER – Committee of Permanent Representatives (Comite des Representants Permanents)
COSI – Committee on Internal Security
CSI – Container Security Initiative
DG – Directorate General
DHS – Department of Homeland Security
EC – European Commission
EDPS – European Data Protection Supervisor
EGF – European Gendarmerie Force
EP – European Parliament
ESDP – European Security and Defence Policy
ESRIF – European Security Research and Innovation Forum
ESTA – Electronic System for Travel Authorisation
EU – European Union
EU MIS – European Union Law Enforcement Information Management Strategy
EUPM – European Union Police Missions
FBI – Federal Bureau of Investigation
FIU – Financial Intelligence Unit
FRONTEX – European Agency for the Management of Operational Cooperation at the External Borders
G8 – Group of Eight
GMES – Global Monitoring for Environment and Security
GUE – Confederal Group of the European United Left
ID – Identity
IOM – International Organisation on Migration
IP – Internet Protocol

IPU – Integrated Police Units
ISP – Internet Service Providers
JHA – Justice and Home Affairs
JLS – Justice, Freedom and Security (Commission)
LEA – Law Enforcement Agency
LIBE – Committee on Civil Liberties, Justice and Home Affairs
MDG – Multidisciplinary Group on Organised Crime (Council Working Party)
MIC – Monitoring and Information Centre
MLA – Mutual Legal Assistance
MOU – Memorandum of Understanding
NATO – North Atlantic Treaty Organisation
NSA – National Security Agency
NTA – New Transatlantic Agenda
OJ – Official Journal of the European Union
PCCC – Police and Customs Cooperation Centres
PET – Privacy Enhancing Technologies
PNR – Passenger Name Record
POA – Principle of Availability
PSE – Party of European Socialists (Parti Socialiste Européen)
RABITS – Rapid Border Intervention Teams
RFID – Radio Frequency Identification
RPP – Regional Protection Programmes
SEMDOC – Statewatch European Monitoring and Documentation Centre
SIS – Schengen Information System
SWIFT – Society for Worldwide Interbank Financial Telecommunication
TNI – Transnational Institute
UK – United Kingdom
UN – United Nations
USA – United States of America
US – United States
VIS – Visa Information System
VWP – Visa Waiver Programme

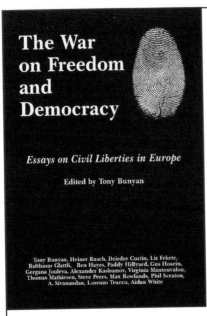
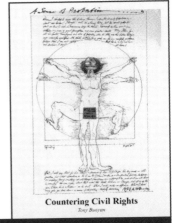